The Inner Journey

by Christophe Javon

GRATITUDE

I would like to express deep gratitude to all my teachers and to all those who have touched my heart. May their gifts continually bloom.

In particular, I would like to express a heartfelt thank you to my teacher Max Christensen for the amazing gifts he so generously offers. He is a true treasure-giver of keys for self-awakening. Although he always refuses credit and simply says, "you did it all yourself," he has expanded my life and helped me find the treasures within myself that I had been looking for all along.

Also, I am deeply grateful to Donna Bradley for all her teachings and support throughout the years I've known her.

Special thanks and appreciation to my amazing editor, Smita Khatri for her invaluable help.

To my wife Janet, my children Ayden and Alyza, and their love, now and always. They are my true teachers.

DISCLAIMERS

Please always follow your own truth. Use the information covered in this book at your own discretion and enjoyment.

None of the information I share is intended to replace medical advice for any condition.

I simply seek to share my experiences and what could be inspiring to the interested reader.

Nothing should be inferred as a description, even in minute parts, of Max Christensen's KUNLUN® System.

However, I wish to provide reference to his book *KUNLUN® System, The Path of Inner Alchemy Leading to the Truth Within.*

Any misinterpretations of his system that could transpire through my writings, after a mere few years of practice, are purely my own.

CONTENTS

Preface   xiii

Part 1: It's Only The Beginning

The Inner Journey, an Introduction   3

The Riddle of the Mind   11

The Spiritual Quest 1   17

My Story in Brief   19

This Present Moment   33

Refinement of Emotions   37

Unlocking the Intelligence of the Heart   49

Reality Shifts   53

The Practice of Giving and Taking   69

Self-Love   77

To Love is Divine   87

The Fruit of Silence   89

Love and Alchemy   91

Compassion   93

Miracles   95

Prayer   105

The Inner Journey, It's Just the Beginning   107

Part 2: Going Deeper

Preface   119

Introduction   121

The Spiritual Quest 2   127

The Wish-fulfilling Gem   129

Stillness   131

Pearls of Light   133

Shortcuts to Awakening   135

Forgetting   137

Spiritual Emergency   139

Self-Inquiry and Objective Reality   141

What Do You See?   143

The Gift   147

The Veils of the Mind   149

Ode to Silence   151

Anger 1   155

Anger 2   157

Waking up from the Dream 1   159

Waking up from the Dream 2   161

Merging Divine Feminine and Divine Masculine 1   163

Merging Divine Feminine and Divine Masculine 2   165

Self-Acceptance   167

Individualized Particle of God   169

World Peace 1   171

The Mirror of Relationships   175

Paths to the Divine   177

Embracing our Limitations   181

Shortcomings 1   185

Shortcomings 2   187

Facing Our Fear
     (Transmuting Fear Back Into Grace)   189

On Grieving   195

Releasing Old Subconscious Programming   197

Ordinary Miracles   205

The Middle Path 207

We Are One 209

When Giving and Receiving Cannot be Distinguished 213

The Object of Devotion, The Radiance of Our True Nature
The End of Suffering, War and Violence
or How to Turn Darkness Into Light 217

Bring The Mind To Peace 221

World Peace 2 223

Keeping Things Simple 225

Purification 227

Mindset 229

The Dance of Perfection
Unbearable Exquisite Sweetness 231

The Dance of Perfection
Practice: 7 minutes of stillness 233

The Cave Retreat 1 237

Letting Go 239

The Cave Retreat 2 243

The Cave Retreat 3 245

Free Yourself Into Truth 247

Giving Thanks 249

Part 3: Returning To The Beginning

Nosedive   253

Meditation Journal   255

The Cocoon Phase   261

Everything is Vibration   263

Finding Balance   265

I'm Almost There   267

Healers   269

Song to the Divine   271

Song of Freedom   273

PREFACE

Twenty-five years ago, I started to journal to gain clarity and understanding about the crisis I was going through at the time. I was writing my doctoral thesis in physics and found myself at a big turning point. What did I really want to do next? Where was I, really, at this point in my life? Most importantly, the crisis was pointing with urgent clarity at the life force that I felt was held repressed inside of me. It felt very much like a facade crumbling – the facade of being nice and polite. The mask of pretending to be okay.

The feelings and buried issues, suddenly bursting to the surface, were so intense that I had to seek help.

I must have tried ten different professionals. Psychiatrists did not seem to care, and merely suggested medication. Psychoanalysts seemed strange and mysterious, if not plain quirky.

I eventually found a psychologist who radiated human warmth. He was caring, and immediately showed an ability to tune into what I was experiencing. I could hardly find words for the flood of feelings that overwhelmed me. The psychologist encouraged me to write, so at least I'd have something to work with at our sessions.

Over time, I started to gain clarity and put some pieces of the puzzle of my own psyche together. After nine months of attending sessions regularly, a series of big catharses came through my writings. When I shared them with my therapist, he said, "wow, you must publish a book someday."

That was many years ago, the beginning of my inner quest.

Through my humble experiences, I have gained a number of shifts in perspective. Those are the fruits I want to share.

You will find that this book is about love. Love as I feel it today. But also love as universal principle. Love as the source as well as the manifestations of our existence. Love as integrated spirituality – the merging of the divine with our individual selves. But more about that later…

Through sharing some of my experiences, I mainly want to convey to you an appreciation for the Great Mystery within yourself and all around you. May this appreciation be a positive catalyst for the transformations you desire.

Throughout these writings, I use terms such as "meditation" or "spiritual practices" to cover a wide range of activities, such as traditional meditation, prayer, self-inquiry, feeling, devotion, contemplation, inner energy cultivation, just to name a few. May this book be of some use to all, regardless of spiritual path and beliefs.

At this point, I cannot separate my personal journey from my desire to inspire others in the ways my various teachers have inspired me.

I must again express my gratitude to Max Christensen, who generously shares practices for self-awakening with anyone willing to learn. In the past, these practices were kept secret, empowering only the few dedicated students willing to go through the preliminary austerities of monastic and yogic life.

I met Max in 2008 during one of his introductory lectures. It came at the perfect moment in my life; I was thirsty for anything that would raise my vibration, as long as it felt real and authentic. Everything he said on that day of our first meeting has proven true in my life today.

I cannot convey how empowering it was to be in his presence. What struck me was how fun, lively and personal he was. He had none of the seriousness and decorum we tend to associate with spiritual discourse. He actually radiated such strong energy that many in the audience went into spontaneous experience or visible bliss. I, myself, was buzzing at recognizing the truths he spoke.

The method he offers is so simple that I only had to see him once to start the process of self-awakening within myself, and I immediately felt it. Through his radiant presence, he opened me up to the "path of no more learning". This simply refers to the stage where one no longer learns by adding more "stuff," but rather, by letting go of past conditioning and opening up to the truth within. It is more a process of tuning in to our own perfection that is already there: a process of allowing, not forcing.

The method, that he named KUNLUN® System, is totally self-teaching. It taps into the truth that we already have all the necessary chemistry within our bodies to access and open up to our most divine essence.

Through a formless form, we learn to re-open the energy body and remember our true spiritual essence.

Max simply says, "You are your own teacher, your own beginning and your own end."

For a description of the KUNLUN® System, including its ancient roots and history as well as the methods, please refer to Max's book. You will find amazing keys for self-awakening.

Gone are the days when you could not make significant spiritual progress without a Guru. Remember, a Guru, a true master, is like a mirror to you; he or she shows you your true potential, shows you what is possible. Everything else is still all up to you.

The Inner Journey

Part 1   It's Only The Beginning

The Inner Journey, an Introduction

Let's start with energy.

You must already know that everything is energy. Matter is energy, thoughts are energy, love is energy, light is energy.

Energy moves things. If you have an idea with little passion in it, you won't accomplish much. If the idea is sustained by love and passion, you can move mountains.

In the "doing without doing" state that mystics talk about, you have surrendered so completely to the magnetic flow of the universe, running as the love that sustains you, that the physical manifestations others see as miracles are mere trifles to you.

In its purest form, energy is pure potential, the energy of creation. Different traditions have different names for it. They may call it the un-manifest, the unborn or the Holy Spirit. It is the formless present within all forms, the original void-space. Please set aside all labels, even for just a moment, and you will see the unity in all things.

One hundred years ago, Einstein proposed the concept of zero-point energy, nowadays affectionately called quantum-vacuum-zero-point energy by new age people and scientists alike. Scientists have established this energy to be virtually infinite, all pervasive. We are not aware of it because, like fish in the water, we swim in this energy inside and out so it is in perfect balance everywhere.

When energy comes into form, it is never stagnant. Energy is motion. Look at the source of energy that started the industrial era – steam. Where does steam come from? Hot water. What happens to water when it is heated? The molecules move faster and faster until the molecular bonds break. The resulting bubbles of steam spring up to the surface and fly off.

What is that thing bubbling to the surface inside of you? It is love, of course. Where is its source? In every cell, every nucleus and every atom of your body.

You may know that to probe the sub-particles of the atomic nucleus, physicists must use higher and higher energies. They are trying to probe the past by recreating the temperature conditions of the early universe, reaching higher and higher temperatures.

At that scale of the infinitely small, matter, which is simply a pattern of vibration of the void-space, vibrates incredibly fast.

This is the same matter found in your body. I used to think, my goodness, if physicists keep doing that (smashing atoms at higher and higher energies), they are one day going to create a whole new universe and obliterate this one.

In your body, there is enough energy to create whole new universes!

You don't want to do that just yet because your body would disintegrate. So you use only this tiny, tiny portion of your energy in order to have this physical experience.

But you can learn to harness more energy within the physical body, which means teaching your body to handle more energy without getting zapped.

In my understanding thus far of the spiritual path, the reason why we're here is to learn to bring all this energy, this divine potential, down into the physical body.

Advanced spiritual practitioners can increase their vibration to the point of converting matter into pure energy, and back into physical form. In the tradition that I learned from my teachers, this attainment is called the Golden Dragon Body. At this level, the practitioner hangs around as long as he or she can be of service to humanity, and then moves on. I call that graduation.

Everybody will graduate, so why worry? Enjoy that experience while you're here, and learn what you have to learn. If you live your life well, you will leave a trail of light behind you that others can use on their path.

The paradox is that in order to awaken to higher rates of vibration, we must let go of our usual agitation, which uses only the surface of our energy system. Through stillness, we can reach deeper levels lying dormant within ourselves.

When we quiet the chatter of the busy mind, sometimes called the mundane mind or monkey mind, we can touch the energy of the void, opening us up to the deeper and unseen aspects of reality.

In some spiritual circles there is such a preoccupation with ascension. You actually came here to embody this infinite light, to bring this love down into a physical body. Over-preoccupation with ascension is just another form of running away from yourself.

To give you an idea about energy, once I felt a surge passing through me as if a 10,000-volt electric shock had hit me. Yet I felt vibrantly alive and in a state of bliss. On another occasion, one of these electric surges pushed me about ten feet back without touching the ground and then across the room (there were many witnesses). It actually felt as if I had put my hands in an electrical socket and was then pushed back for my own protection. Once, I felt so much energy during a group class that I had to run outside; I instinctively walked barefoot on the earth and hugged a tree without knowing or questioning why – a phenomenon I now know is simply your body's instinct for grounding. On a few occasions, a spontaneous fire breath took over, feeling so easy and natural compared to the forced version of fire breathing. I have also had numerous experiences of spontaneous suspension of the breath.

All of the above experiences resulted in a deeper state of peace and joy; and new understandings about myself emerged.

Now, I am nothing special. Or rather, I should say that everybody is the same yet special in their own way. All of the experiences I described above were temporary side effects that I experienced with the KUNLUN® System. I only mention them here so you understand that there are tangible effects that are not just subjective. These effects are not what is important to me. Remember, everybody's experiences are different and uniquely individual. Learn to trust your own ways.

It doesn't matter to me so much what you do, only that you love what you do and do what you love.

I see all paths as equivalent. Your guidelines are within – that is the love, joy, sincerity and grace that you carry. This is the self-teaching process we call life.

Now, since this book is the fruit of subjective experiences directly related to inner explorations, I'd like to mention here that I do not do drugs and neither do I advocate the use of them.[1] I don't condemn them either, because I respect the beautiful ways of many ancient shamanic and tribal traditions. In many tribes, the medicine man is the one who can see the root of diseases and foster their cure, communicate with nature and gather the healing plants, travel through worlds and bring back information from the invisible realms.

However, it would be incorrect to think that such experiences are accessible only through mind-altering substances.

Of course, I've had a few isolated experiences to know some of the effects of some common drugs – ranging from mildly entertaining, to very insightful, to terrifying.

When you have a drug-induced experience, you know that you haven't earned it through your own efforts and dedication.

When you have an experience through a meditative or self-explorative method, it usually opens you up to the next octave of vibration, as compared to your "normal" everyday state of consciousness. That dissonance is what actually propels you to make changes in your life; and gradually, your outer reality matches your inner reality and you become the embodiment of your highest state of awareness all the time, not just during meditation.

---

[1] *However, I do not want to dismiss sacred plants and substances used for medicinal or therapeutic purposes. I am aware of their healing potential for certain conditions. I just don't have the personal experience to talk about it.*

Throughout history, many have reached the supreme attainment – God realization, Self-realization, Body of Light, Body of Grace, Body of Wisdom, Rainbow Body, Golden Dragon Body, merging with the Tao, the Great Mystery. There are infinite variations of the infinite; actually, as many as there are individuals.

Those who have reached the exalted state are people like you and me who, through their exemplary path, have merged their hearts with the divine in service to humanity. And they all have the same message, which is to follow the truth within yourself. The greatest gifts are waiting within.

Study the lives of saints if you'd like. You will find that in between their work of service, they disappear and go into retreat, sometimes for days, months or even years at a time.

What do they do in retreat?

They sit in silence to drink at the fountain of truth that can only be found within. Anybody can do that. The saint is just like you and me, but he sets the path of what is possible by his example.

The saint is not trying to be a saint. He is not trying to be like another saint. He is just committed to being his true self, an embodiment of radiant truth. Anybody can do that. You don't have to do anything else but be yourself. You can call that a God-given gift if you'd like; it is still the simplest thing in the world.

Interestingly, the fountain of truth is also called the fountain of youth because the saint will regain a youthful glow. There are many documented stories of enlightened masters whose bodies did not decay after death and whose skin retained elasticity for a long time. Incidentally, the greatest saints do not leave a body behind, but I'll leave that up to you to research.

Now, to come back to the subject of drugs, a drug may propel you 2 or 3 octaves of vibration higher. This comes at a price, though. You don't know how to integrate the "higher planes" into your life.

It is very unlikely that you will know afterward how to have the experience without the drug (which is what attracted you to the drug in the first place – you wanted a taste of something you thought you could not have without a boost). This may result in dependency and addiction. You remain somewhat disconnected, separate from your highest realizations. The crash, the return to your mundane mind, can be brutal and you may find yourself lower than from where you started, with a fragmented psyche.

You should know that all drugs simply mimic the natural chemicals that your body, in its timeless wisdom, knows how to produce. Your body is simply waiting for you to gently release these chemicals – hormones and neurotransmitters – through your endocrine and nervous systems during your natural and spontaneous experiences.

For example, you may have heard of serotonin, the "feel good" neurotransmitter naturally produced when you're in love or when you're happy. Many drugs work by boosting your serotonin levels. Tryptophan, an amino acid precursor to serotonin, is found in many foods, such as bananas and raw chocolate. Another important neurotransmitter, dopamine, is involved with the pain and pleasure centers within the brain. For this reason, many substances that affect the dopamine circuits are highly addictive. The same is true of all habit-forming behaviors.

It is better to produce the natural chemistry for motivation; simply ask yourself what you really want in life, and then live it and be it.

Endorphins, the natural painkillers of the body, are produced during intense athletic activities, especially when you push your limits. Everybody knows the benefits of exercise, and that there is more joy in doing it than in watching sports on TV.

DMT, the so-called spirit molecule, is actually a compound naturally produced by the pineal gland during intense spiritual experiences, feelings of oneness, and opening to the unseen aspects of reality.

With a drug, you may get an illusory awakening, thinking you have reached the top, but this actually blocks you from further progress on your spiritual path.

What is the top?

Some traditions say there are 100 levels of perception, or levels of reality. In truth, who can say where it stops?

At what point do you say, "Well, I think this is enough oneness, enough love, enough joy, enough compassion, enough wisdom and clarity… I think I'll stop here"?

When a saint reaches the summit, he will tell you that he feels like a child at the doorstep of infinity and that it is just the beginning.

The Riddle of the Mind

The spiritual quest is filled with apparent paradoxes.

There is a level at which all paradoxes disappear.

You must have heard the saying, in order to be full one has to become empty.

Such paradox is no paradox at all if you realize that in order to observe your mind, you must use your mind. To experience yourself, you have to be it.

Let me give you a very simple example. You can analyze love all you want, but unless you feel love, unless you are love, you cannot really understand what love is. Or if you want to understand what a tree is, you have to be the tree.

What could be more important than understanding yourself? Understanding others, you could say. Yet wouldn't we comprehend and accept others better if we really knew ourselves?

A little self-inquiry will quickly reveal that to understand our own mind is not that easy. You can observe others, but then you have an external understanding.

You can observe yourself, but from what viewpoint do you do that?

From the center? From the circumference? From everywhere? Who is observing? What is being observed? What is the mind?

Are you your mind?

Are you your thoughts? Your feelings? A byproduct of your body? Are you your cells, when each has a life of its own that goes on independently of your will?

Are you your hopes and dreams? Your wants and desires?

Are you your virtues and your weaknesses? Are you the emptiness between your thoughts? Are you your experiences?

Are you limited, are you unlimited?

In its pure essence, isn't the mind all of these and yet much more?

You can turn yourself blue with all these questions and continue ad infinitum. Some meditation practices, such as systematic self-inquiry, actually aim at that. You exhaust the seeking mind until it finally gives up, exposing the radiant truth.

How does it work? The way I see it is that to define the mind with the mind is a sort of paradoxical self-reference of the mind trying to grasp itself. It is the symbol of the snake swallowing its tail that is found in many ancient traditions.

Let me give you an analogy. Analogies have their limits, but they can trigger new perspectives. Also, analogies can be more than just analogies. They can be the "hidden" hints to the repeating patterns seen throughout the universe. These patterns are present at every scale of creation, from the microscopic to the cosmic. You must know that when you look at the beautiful Milky Way across a dark night sky, you are looking at our own galaxy. Now since we are right in the smack of it, and stars are so distant from us, it appears as if this band of stars is separate from us, while the stars closest to us appear scattered around the celestial sphere.

With the mind, it is a bit the same.[2] I cannot name an experience that is not the mind since all experiences arise in the mind. From the most mundane and physical experience, to the most transcendental and ethereal, it is still the mind. Now from that perspective, you can see that your view of the mind will start to enlarge and encompass more.

Now, if I say, "observe your mind," notice a feeling of contraction and a certain coldness, a disconnection. If I say, "Be it, live it," then you are more likely to have a feeling of expansion, of warmth, of aliveness.

Lately, everybody raves about quantum physics. Scientists have finally figured out that you can never separate what is being observed from what is observing.

Whenever you observe a system, you are always part of that system, so you affect it. There is no such thing as objective observation. By observing, you immediately change the system with all its dynamics.

Can you step outside the mind to observe it? No. Observing is a

---

[2] *Interestingly, the order of magnitude (in the hundred of billions) of the number of neurons in the human brain is comparable to the number of stars in the Milky Way, as well as the "estimated" total number of galaxies in the "known" universe. This may hint at the relevance of the analogy.*

mere activity of the mind. To observe the mind, you have to stop observing and be the whole. You have to stop separating into subject and object. You have to become the whole.

In merely observing, you may miss the point. The point of life is to experience life, to be it.

Paradoxes are lifted when you stop identifying yourself with the "small self", and remember the "big self", the oneness from which you came. You are a spark of the divine, in all its variations and infinite manifestations!

Like the masters say, the mind's original nature is already there, perfect; you cannot add to it, you cannot remove from it.

Rest into the mind's perfection, into your own perfection; everything else is just stories.

The truth is that it is so simple, so liberating, so freeing; all one can do is laugh about it, or melt in tears of joy and tenderness!

The paradox is that although our perfection is already there and nothing needs to be done to make it better, our finite mind (the "monkey mind") likes to feel like that it is making progress towards it. In order to remember its original nature, the mind must regain its spaciousness rather than identify itself with the various waves that agitate it. This is why stillness is considered a key in many spiritual systems.

The beauty of stillness is that it is bountiful and available to all. In stillness, the pristine clarity of the true nature of the mind reveals itself, and the intuitive intelligence of the heart is awakened. The open heart becomes like an open book to the whole universe, making oneness between all things a tangible experience.

Individuality and oneness are not contradictory, for individuality is just the viewpoint from which you observe...actually, the viewpoint from which you are this universe.

The Spiritual Quest 1

Seeking is the natural process that pulls us back towards our own magnificence, in and as the beauty of this present moment.

In order to truly see and feel what's there, you have to stop seeking and simply feel and see what's there, in this present moment.

The ineffable beauty, the intensity, the infinite nature of it cannot be put into words. Yet its simplicity, emptiness and luminosity are mind-boggling.

Every religion, every spiritual tradition tries to name it, to own it. But in truth, it cannot be named and it cannot be owned.

Yet it is the crown of the human experience.

It is the same for all, yet ever expanding, for who can say he has achieved it with a final word?

This is why we are all the same. No one higher, no one lower. No matter what your path is and where you consider yourself to be on your cosmic scale of evolution, the peak of your experience is still to see and feel what is there now.

This is what is meant by "the beginning and the end are one and the same."

My Story in Brief

For as long as I can remember, I always had a deep love for learning. Every new school year, I would contemplate the topics in my textbooks and could not wait to learn all this cool new stuff. Everything to learn was a source of wonder and excitement for me, except history lessons, which I could hardly relate to because none of them felt relevant to how real people think and feel. I got along pretty well with most of my teachers, but for some reason, I never clicked with the history teachers and I must have given them a pretty hard time, as these were the classes in which I tended to get into trouble the most. I enjoyed very much making other kids laugh, even if it meant getting reprimanded for it on occasions.

I loved to look at the starry night sky, and ponder the mysteries of existence and the universe in its infinite vastness.

I ended up pursuing that passion all the way. No, I did not become a cosmonaut although as a kid I wanted to. But I got a PhD in thermonuclear physics.

Besides my love for the cosmos and my existential questions on life and death (mostly in the form of anxieties I could not resolve), I would say my inner journey had its roots as a child when I saw a documentary on Bruno Bettelheim, a doctor who dedicated his life to helping autistic children. I was deeply moved by seeing an adult put so much care into understanding those children who have built seemingly insurmountable fortresses around themselves.

This later developed into an interest in psychology, the mysteries of the subconscious and its potential for healing.

My mother was a beautiful soul, a kind, generous and deeply compassionate spirit. She took care of our old great aunt who suffered from rather severe paranoia and various hallucinations. My mother dedicated a good deal of her energy spending time with our old aunt after work, cooking for her and doing her household chores. Thanks to my mom's help and support, our aunt was able to stay in her home until the age of 97, despite all the afflictions from which she suffered.

I was often impressed by my mother's genuine compassion. She would never pass a homeless person without giving them something, a smile and a kind word. If we did not finish our food, she would have a sincere outcry of grief about wasting food. "Some people are starving in the world and don't have food on their plate," she would say with a heartfelt tone. If we threw a candy wrapper in the street or on the subway in Paris, she would pick it up with a similar outcry out of concern for the next street sweeper who would have to pick up for our carelessness.

Our family situation weighed down on her and her mood was always depressed and unhappy with the recurring theme being her constant longing for my father. The only time I remember her not being unhappy was when she played the piano – she was quite a virtuoso.

They had great love for each other and maintained their relationship throughout my childhood. They worked together and, when coming home, always showed great love and affection for each other until my father would leave to catch his train for the suburbs. My father was previously married and chose to never end his relationship with his wife out of fear of her vengeful reaction, or so they said. It wasn't completely unfounded, as she did once show up at their office with a gun.

My father was a brilliant man who one could call a "genius."

In his childhood, he was moved 9 grades in 3 years. He had extraordinary photographic memory. He knew word for word all the pages of all his textbooks, to the great frustration of his teachers. On the first day of each school year, he could not understand why the teacher would keep asking such easy questions; the answers were already on page so and so.

He took advantage of his abilities during his years in captivity as a prisoner of war during WWII. He was a translator. He could entertain his bunker by memorizing a dictionary. His mates would tell him the first word of a page, and he could recite the rest of the page with all the definitions.

In his youth, he was also an accomplished athlete in many disciplines.

My father did not need sleep like everybody else. He took a few 1-hour naps throughout the day, and could dispense altogether of night sleep.

(Interestingly, I have found such an increase in energy with my spiritual practices that my sleep patterns have greatly changed. This becomes very handy when you want to pursue your passions and really be there and enjoy your family. I tend to have energy crashes in the afternoon, but for the most part I marvel at being okay with the sleepless nights, being awaken regularly, and getting up early – things that come with the territory in parenthood.)

Years of severe malnutrition while in captivity, followed by years of heavy smoking, took a toll on my father's mental feats, according to him. However, he still joked that being in a restaurant could be slightly overwhelming. What we heard as indistinct chatter around us, he could hear as simultaneous, distinct, multiple conversations. Then he would amuse us by proving it on the spot.

I remember him as a jovial, bright spirit who always lifted people's moods in social situations.

I, of course, greatly missed being able to be closer to him, to actually know him and truly connect with him.

My brother was also a very bright, creative and willful spirit. The family situation also weighed on him, and I took the brunt of his anger, rage and frustrations.

The hard part was not so much when he made a deep cut in my arm just to show me how sharp his new knife was, but more the daily insults and put downs throughout my childhood. Over the years, I lost the ability to defend myself, afraid of what I'd say or do that would make him mad; and I started to believe everything he said.

This pushed me towards withdrawal and a rather fearful disposition with low self-esteem, to a point where I consider myself to have been autistic during my teenage years, for developmental reasons (not genetic).

I love who I am today and I appreciate how every experience contributed to that. I have great compassion for my brother's pain.

Today, he is a beautiful young grandfather with loving children and grandchildren. One of my nephews is a French champion of Karate.

My mother died when I was 18. A mid-life crisis, with its potential for healing and positive changes, was completely misunderstood by the professionals from whom she sought help. A serious nervous breakdown led her to a suicide attempt, which shattered my illusion of being able to make her life brighter. It is unbelievable to me that the medical profession still uses electric shock treatments, which also had its days in America to treat the achings of the heart and mental breakdowns. They used a shorter and "low intensity" version of the shock for which they had the euphemism of electro-narcose. Her depression went away, but so did her personality. She came out of it very confused, with no memory and poor muscle control. It was very painful to see her unable to write down simple things, or to play the piano. She ended up falling down a set of stairs and hitting her head. She was in a coma for a week before she passed away.

I can still remember that shock vividly. My withdrawal got deeper and I spent many years in complete isolation, in a state of quasi-amnesia, completely forgetting the past and pretending to be okay and live a normal life (which I secretly thought would be impossible for me). While taking classes at the university, I regularly fell asleep, unable to maintain my attention. I was completely unable to relate to any of my peers.

What saved me was that I maintained a passion for rock climbing and spent a lot of time in nature.

I consider it a miracle that I recovered from that period of isolation and learned to gradually open myself to others.

When I met my first girlfriend, my inability to talk and express myself was definitely a hindrance to our relationship. After a couple weeks, she told me she couldn't help me and she ended our relationship. Of course, little does she know that she saved my life. The crisis was so intense; the loneliness I had tried to adapt to for many years suddenly felt so unbearable that I had to seek help.

In my first journal, I wrote, "the idea that the love that is enclosed within my heart will stay there buried forever is unbearable."

After some time, I decided to come to Los Angeles to do primal therapy, and gradually relearned to access my feelings and reopen the flow of life force held within me.

I not only went through this therapy for myself, but also studied it with dedication to become a primal therapist (although I did not accomplish this goal because I wasn't interested in getting the necessary degrees in traditional psychology required by state law).

The kindness and sensitivity of my therapist, as well as her intelligence and ability to show me understanding and compassion, even in my most withdrawn states, is what really helped me open up and break the walls of what I call my autism.

It was during this time in primal therapy that I met my first wife, Jana. During our 15 years of relationship, we helped each other tremendously with facing and healing our traumas. She was a magnetic, wild and free spirit who left a deep impression on everyone who knew her. She tended to set the tone of our relationship because, unfortunately, I was still very repressed. I tended to be too serious and wasn't very good at having fun.

Jana grew up with a psychotic mother who beat her ritualistically every single day of her entire childhood, rain or shine. On one Christmas day, her mom was about to administer the daily beating with the Christmas tree; but the tree hit the ceiling, which saved her, only to get her regular beating instead. She lived in a small room with closed shutters, no sunlight, no toys and no TV. Her mom would take her on regular trips across America to distribute religious pamphlets, with hardly any money for commodities. Once, they ran out of gas in the middle of the desert and Jana's mom stayed there petrified. Jana, then 9 years old, had to leave her mom and the car behind to go seek help and avoid death by dehydration.

Jana was a survivor. When she was 12, she took her mom to court to emancipate herself. Prior to that, she got her last beating and her mom pulled dice on her to ask god whether or not she should kill her.

I think what saved her was her determination to stay in touch with her feelings and her compassionate heart, and not give up on her understanding of what is right and what is wrong, which she had to establish for herself at a very early age in a way that most of us never have to face.

Her compassion, ability to heal others, and artistic visions were amazing. Much of her art expressed the intensities of the abuse of her childhood and her desire to make the world a more loving place.

The years of abuse took their toll on her body. All her life, she suffered from severe chronic illnesses and conditions, aggravated by the plethora of medications she was prescribed. When she fell gravely ill, she could not even get her body to absorb nourishment properly. Doctors recommended a surgery that would have left her very incapacitated. She no longer felt the level of pain with her physical body was acceptable.

I had tremendous love and compassion for her and I did the best I could.

I remember one awakening experience that was deeply moving for me. She was struggling with her pain and I suddenly saw and told her, "You are love." It was beyond you are loved, everything will be okay, don't give up hope. It was this very deep understanding, this vision, that beyond all pain, you are actually love itself. During these last 6 months, I took care of her the best I could before she took her own life.

In her last letter to me and to her close ones, she made me promise to not hold her back, to let her go to the light and be free and happy. Her final words, recorded in a fading handwriting, were, *"love each other and show them that you love them, my last words."*

I took her assignment to heart and used the intense grieving period to work as deeply as I could on myself to transcend her loss.

I delved into spiritual practices with the intent to raise my vibration and lift the veil of illusion of separation. I called that sacred grief because I wanted to transmute her loss into something golden. I allowed it to bring me closer to the divine so that I could understand where she is.

I took for granted that I would hear from her after her death because she seemed so connected to the other side while she was alive. For instance, when she lived in Venice Beach, prior to knowing me, she experienced a period of time when ghosts lined up to visit her and sought her help – very similar to scenes from the movie *The Sixth Sense*. Once, after getting the name of one of her visitors, she asked her landlord, "Do you know this person?" The landlord said, "Yes, she lived here and died a few years ago."

But all those who have experienced grief know that the first stage is to be faced with this enormous hole, this unbearable emptiness. (Although, every grieving process is deeply personal so your experience may be different than mine.)

A lot of my healing involved facing the different waves of pain, regret and guilt for all the moments when I had not been able to allow the flow of love and joy to bring us back to happiness.

I was fortunate to have a great support group. I attended retreats and classes with Donna Bradley. Donna is one of those saintly beings who radiate such a presence of unconditional love and wisdom from the heart.[3]

To me, Donna is the embodiment of the Divine Mother. Her simplicity, wisdom and love are compelling. Many years before opening the Radiance Healing Center where I met her, Donna and her husband, Joe, adopted (or took long-term guardianship of) seventeen very special children and then went on to create sanctuary for another twenty or more children whose families were

---

[3] *Interestingly, I was introduced to Donna a few years back by Jana. The way Jana found Donna is worth mentioning. Jana sometimes used kinesiology (muscle testing) as a way of communicating with her guidance. One day, she was given a complete street name with directions. So she just showed up, and Donna was there at the doorstep and said to her: "I have been waiting for you, my dear." I later heard from Donna herself that this kind of thing is not at all uncommon for her.*

in crisis. Almost all of their children had experienced abandonment, neglect, brain and other physical injury due to fetal drug exposure, molestation, starvation and loss. And yet, as Donna writes on her website, "love and healing and laughter and joy flowed even as old trauma and pain was released and healed. These children came through our home blessing us with their courage and their hearts. I was often in awe that a child could go through such trauma and arrive on our doorstep still looking for love. Their vulnerable hearts broke our hearts open."

Many went to Donna's healing center, attracted to her light and her ability to draw the love and wisdom from all the lessons we go through. I saw many transform in the mere presence of her radiance.

I experienced many openings and personal transformations during her retreats. I am eternally grateful for her presence in my heart.

The healing journey took me beyond anything I could have imagined. Over time, a passion emerged: the profound desire to help others realize the amazing gifts and treasures that await them within.

It was after a year of spending at least two hours a day with various healing and spiritual practices, that I met Max. I was deeply impressed with his views on life and death, and his simple yet powerful approach for awakening and transcending the veils of illusion of separation. It was clear to me that he was offering a simple practice for enlightenment, so to speak, accessible to everyone regardless of the life they choose for themselves.

It was new to me that such a method is available, and that it is not necessary to go to a remote temple in the Himalayas, or retreat in a cave, to accomplish the highest goal. At least, that is what Max conveyed with his powerful, radiant, lively and fun presence. He made everything sound so simple, and I must give him credit for transmitting what he learned through a lifetime of spiritual dedication in a way that is completely stripped of unnecessary dogma.

He was touring then, and I could not study with him right away. So I started with the book he had published at the time. Also, I was fortunate that Rich Romer and Mary Pirtle were offering classes on Maui. Because they both studied intensely with Max, I learned many things that they had learned directly from him as well as from their personal practices and life journeys. I am very grateful to both of them.

Much beautiful unfolding came during this time.

As I learned to reopen myself to the outside world and went through my transformations, I was magically guided to my wife Janet.

She was on vacation on Maui and we met just two days before it was time for her to fly back to Los Angeles. Our connection was instantaneous, and there was an implicit and mutual understanding that of course we were going to be together and spend our lives together.

She gave me a card reading on the beach, and before I had a chance to share much, she saw that I had just been through a major loss and was going through a major spiritual transformation.

We connected on everything – black holes, the energy of the void, oneness and spirit, joy and creativity, the evolution of consciousness. I saw the strength of her spirit in her dedication to the spiritual path and service from an early age.

Before she flew back to Los Angeles, her girlfriends teased her, "Uh-oh…you're moving to Maui, girlfriend."

For the next couple months, before I could visit her in Los Angeles, we talked on the phone every day, sometimes for three to four hours; often we read Hafiz's poetry to each other into the late hours of the night.

I love her. Her sparkling smile and joyful presence always light up my heart as if for the first time. It never ceases to touch me and move me. I am so grateful for all the opportunities we have to share our excitement and joy for discovery, self-growth and creativity.

I could not be sharing all this with you if it wasn't for her love and support. She helps me be a better man. She reminds me of how much I have opened up since I met her.

I cannot convey the joys of raising our children together. They teach me so much, like how to let go of seriousness and let myself be outrageously present and fun. I think I've made good progress so far, thanks to them. Yesterday my 3-year-old son gave me my first time-out for being too serious; it really helped. The other day, my 1-year-old daughter was holding my head with her little hands, pulling on my cheeks as if to make me smile. She was saying something which at first I could not understand. We adults can be quick to dismiss what infants say as meaningless sounds. Suddenly, I understood she was saying "happy." She gave me quite a transmission of wisdom; it was very humbling and beautiful.

When I go off track, my family calls me Mr. Grumpy Pants. I love them so much.

I live a very simple and fulfilled life. I express my creativity in writing. I also love playing the piano, nurturing my passion for music and beauty. I teach piano, so work is like play to me.

This Present Moment

Blocking off others' feelings with judgments is how we limit ourselves.

Accepting others totally, and embracing ourselves in our full range of expression, is how we shed limitations, re-embrace the full flow of life force, and return to Love and Innocence.

Nobody is ever guilty of limiting you. You only do that to yourself out of fear.

Others are the field of learning for you to experience the full range of your expression, which ultimately is your love, compassion and oneness with all.

As you go through all of your experiences and mind journeys, you seek and you seek, secretly thinking that "later" you will reach something – you will be happy, you will reach enlightenment, you will see the light. The paradox is that when you stop seeking, you finally realize that there is nothing else but enjoying this moment. There is nothing more than exploring and expanding the range of your ability to feel in this moment.

This is the moment of your awakening.

Then every moment is a peak experience that opens to infinite possibilities.

There is only playing in this present moment.

The choice is yours.

Use it well!

What is the most exquisite thing that you can do for yourself right now?

If you find this and remind others of their own magnificence as a side effect of the joy and love that emanates from you, wouldn't that be the greatest gift you can give to anyone?

Limitation is the game we play in order to feel that we are unlimited.

If you were just unlimited, you would be light and that's it. It would be void because you would be stopped at nothing, neither time nor space.

So enjoy your limitations and feel them back into love; this is how you expand back into your infinite nature.

After all is said and done, it matters not how many hours of meditation you do or don't do; neither does it matters how many books you study or what you accomplish. In the end, what matters is how much kindness, grace and inspiration you radiate into this world, in the simplicity of your everyday activities and interactions. What matters is that you engage yourself, heart and soul into what you do.

Life is a creative process that requires our exquisite presence in every moment.

Refinement of Emotions

A natural process unfolds with allowing yourself to feel deeply, to be your true, authentic self.

To feel deeply means to ride your feelings and take them all the way back to their source without judgment or impulsive reactivity. The source is Love. I have never seen an exception to that; therefore this is what I mean when I say the only reality is Love (or at least this is one meaning, for there are deeper levels of truth in that statement).

We are all born as exquisitely sensitive beings. When our needs are not met for too long, or we are made to feel unsafe or unappreciated when we show our true feelings, we learn to adapt, conform and deny some parts of ourselves in order to get by and survive.

Later, as adults, it is not our feelings that cause us suffering but it is our resistance to them. Suffering arises when we resist, avoid or block off altogether feelings that we judge to be unacceptable or deem dangerous because we don't understand them. The paradox is that this process of resisting is what makes the feelings manifest into physical experience, until we have learned the lessons that we were meant to learn.

When you allow yourself to feel, as opposed to go through life "comfortably numbed," you will have phases of great joy and peace, and phases where old buried issues will come to the surface and create turmoil in your life. It's all good. Nothing happens by accident. You are moving towards balance and integration. Everyone is.

When you go through your intensities, overwhelmed with feelings of anger, fear, sadness or grief, say to that difficult feeling (or to the object of your feeling), just like you would say to an abused child whom you would want to comfort, "Please, let me love you, let me hold you in my arms".

Love really is the answer. Always. Your ego will say, "I can't love this, I can't love that!" This is only your ego fighting for survival. It is understandable, but it will only delay your healing. Melt into love, melt all obstacles with love.

You don't have to deny any parts of yourself. It is not only possible to love while honoring your most radiant truth, it is the secret that unties all knots.

You can still use discernment. Let go of the dross but keep the pearl, as the sages say. You will attain clarity. Clarity is here now.

If, instead of feeling your feelings, you choose to act out of anger or fear, and without consideration for the basic needs and rights of others, you will only incur regrets. (Some call this karma, which is simply the consequences to your own choices.) We all have the responsibility to be truthful and to act appropriately to situations that arise in our lives.

Remove the karmic seeds of anger and fear with seeds of truth, gentleness and love. Breathe gently into your belly and let that dissolve all tension and knots stored in your cellular memories of survival. Joy is your birthright!

Once a feeling is experienced fully, it will not present itself again as a block because the lesson has been learned.

Feelings and defense mechanisms can sometimes look alike. True feelings have a ring of truth and simplicity to them. You feel vulnerable, but in that vulnerability, you allow yourself to move closer to what you really want.

With a defense mechanism, you may have a false sense of security because you are keeping what you really want at a distance. Subconsciously, you are afraid that you will not get it, which pushes away what you really want; this, of course, reinforces a negative reality.

It takes a lot of courage to feel your feelings without judgments because our survival mechanisms kick in and we block off certain feelings labeled as negative or unacceptable. We don't want to see those things about ourselves that we worked so hard to push out of ourselves.

But how can we feel the depth of unconditional love that is within us if we block off certain areas of our feelings? We must re-embrace the whole range of our feelings – from fear, sadness and anger to love and joy. We cannot know non-duality if we haven't surrendered to the poles, to all aspects of ourselves.

I remember one of the first things I heard from my teacher, Max: "for every high there is a low." This helped me trust him right away and know that his method was the real deal.

On an intuitive level, everyone can understand this, but what does it really mean for the spiritual aspirant?

The more light you integrate, the more you understand and can reclaim your shadows, which are the parts of yourself you have disconnected from in order to adapt to your environment. Paradoxically, the disconnected parts of yourself control your life to a large extent. That's because it takes a lot of energy to keep them separate. This magnetically attracts the situations in your life that will allow you to heal them. To become whole, you have to re-embrace and love all parts of yourself.

To flow through your feelings without judgment all the way back home doesn't have to be a long and painful process. You simply sit still and stay with your feelings until they bring you back to love.

It takes only a single moment for a turnaround to happen.

It can feel difficult to say the least, to sit still, surrender and let go rather than to try to control and force things. But once you see the magic happening through that single act of slowing down and dropping down into your center, which is found in the stillness, meditation will become effortless and much of the struggle in your life will dissolve.

But you must have the honesty, patience and courage to be still with your feelings until you have returned to love and joy.

Stopping before that is a little bit like digging up a pile of dirty laundry but never finishing it.

An important part of expressing a feeling honestly is focusing on what you really want, rather than on what you don't want.

For me, the best example of that turnaround moment, of the return to love, is the near-death experience in which a person has a meaningful and life changing experience in that single moment of exposure to the light within. (For instance, read the amazing account of Anita Moorjani complete and instant healing from terminal cancer in her book, *Dying To Be Me.*)

After that brief moment of seeing the deeper truth of reality as light and all-encompassing love, they see through their old ways and they see the purpose of their lessons. After that, there is no way they would want to return to attitudes that do not support life-affirming philosophies, joy, self-love and self-empowerment. They have a renewed sense of purpose and appreciation for life, supported by unshakable faith born from direct experience (that is knowledge).

When the near-death experience happens through spiritual practice, my teacher calls this the "little death" experience, which is a form of awakening.

The more "open" you are, the easier it becomes to speak your truth without judgment. And you learn to differentiate between being honest about your feelings and dumping your feelings on someone else. That is, you learn the difference between feelings and "emotional self-indulgence."

Of course everybody will have ups and downs and go through rough times, challenges and lessons. There are times when you have to face your fears. There are times when you are faced with difficult choices. That is not what I'm talking about here. What I am talking about is the indulgence in habitual negative feelings that will spill onto others or even onto our own sense of self. Those habits are so ingrained that we are generally blind to them. We are too immersed in them, too identified with the corresponding feelings. They give us a sense of entitlement into emotional reactivity. They end up being like a baseline that we think of as our "normal" state, but in truth, these emotional habits conceal our true nature from our own awareness.

These habitual responses create a groove and become a pseudo personality, resulting in much drama and negative consequences for others and ourselves. For example, rehashing negative thoughts; being dominated by feelings of anger, hatred, despair and bitterness; resenting others; allowing thoughts of superiority or inferiority to others; being envious of others, being judgmental and controlling – all of these can become habitual patterns that stem from unresolved conflicting feelings. They are defense mechanisms that both point to the lesson we manifested for ourselves and at the same time prevent us from truly learning and moving on to the next stage.

We must always seek responsibility for our own state of mind and remember that we always have a choice about the kind of mindset we want to cultivate.

Self-indulgence in negative emotions is very much like being stuck at the surface of our feelings. It keeps us separate from our real self, which is total freedom in joy, love and compassion.

We must learn to poke through the surface and free ourselves.

Imagine if you suffered an arm injury and you were wearing a cast. The cast serves you for a while, but then if you just forget about it, it will limit you, restrict you and create all sorts of difficulties for you. If you remember it and remove it, you will suddenly feel so free. You will suddenly feel so much lighter, like you were carrying an unnecessary burden.

When we realize that we don't have to perpetuate our habitual thoughts about all the reasons we have to be unhappy, we can suddenly feel so empowered that it's exhilarating. It is very much like finding a switch. Of course I cannot offer you the magic switch. Everyone must find it for themselves. I can only encourage you to do so. For practical purpose, love is the expression of joy and tenderness. Stop blaming others for taking that away from you. Cut if off! Instead allow yourself to be the expression of joy and tenderness, or whatever positive attribute is appropriate for you in the moment. Let it spill onto others. It may take a little effort and willingness at first, but the transformations will blow your mind.

True liberation is not liberation from challenges, conflicts or difficulties, but liberation from the pangs of *reactivity* to extreme emotions like despair, rage, wanting to give up. This freedom is the light everyone is looking for. Free yourself and give this light to others.

A good place to start is to stop worrying and to trust yourself. Be effortless in your efforts for self-improvement – another of those paradoxes of the spiritual path. Be flexible and be kind to yourself so that you can give yourself room to evolve.

With regular introspection, self-inquiry and surrender to your true nature, there is over time a natural and spontaneous process of refinement of emotions, which transmute into higher virtues reflecting a heart that is pure and free of negativities.

To name a few, such virtues include unconditional love, universal compassion, clarity, simplicity, deep joy, peace, contentment, infinite patience, kindness, courage, strength of character, wisdom and humility.

I want to emphasize here that I don't mean virtues as a code of conduct (although there is, of course, virtue in respecting others), but rather, as the highest expression of your true feelings deeply rooted in the innermost essence of your being. Virtues cannot be tainted by outer circumstances, but always shed light on them.

With the refinement of emotions comes refinement of thoughts, which simply means you enjoy your thoughts and don't fight yourself with unwanted thoughts. This is the goal of mastering the self, or mastering the mind, of which many traditions speak.

Remember, do not judge yourself for where you are or where you have been. Everybody does their best at any given time considering what they are aware of at any given moment. There is only learning.

I believe that your feelings are essential for creating the life you want. With a little willingness, and the learning school we call life, thoughts, feelings, words and actions can be in perfect alignment for your benefit and in the best interest of all.

Remember, mindsets and feelings simply reflect our state of alignment within.

The good news here is that positive mindsets are thousands of times more powerful than negative ones.

That is because negativities are a mere symptom of conflict within our psyche; that is parts of us fighting with other parts. On the other hand, positive mindsets embracing joy, love and compassion come out of wholeness and have a unified purpose engaging our synchronized whole being.

The greatest evolutionary driving force in the unfolding of the soul is the return to Love. In spiritual practice, just as in life, every moment is an opportunity to tune in to our perfection and see it in others.

When we are internally in alignment, we have a strong and coherent electromagnetic field that emanates from our body. This is our energy blueprint, our energy signature, so to speak.

When our energy is clear, this magnetic field expands and becomes unified instead of fragmented. What unifies it is the intent held within the heart.

Did you know that scientists have measured that the heart is the organ with the strongest magnetic field? The unified field of the human being is centered on the heart, not the brain.

The Chinese five elements theory is a very good model for observing health or imbalance in our overall energy system. The equivalent can be found in other ancient healing systems such as Ayurveda.

For example, if we are holding repressed anger, magnetic field lines will tighten up around the liver (wood element). The field becomes fragmented into separate magnetic loops. These energy loops are the knots that we may experience as body aches and pains.

If we don't allow joy in our life, the magnetic energy flow will start to contract around the heart (fire), making us feel heavy (weight on the chest) and oppressed rather than light and playful. The shoulders cave in as if to protect us from getting hurt.

If we have difficulties with trusting, or constantly worry about our basic survival needs, we may experience anxiety and symptoms such as a "pit" in the stomach (earth).

With repressed sadness and grief, magnetic loops tighten around the lungs (metal). The tendency to withdraw may manifest as shallow breathing, a way to dim down our life force and avoid painful feelings.

If we allow ourselves to be controlled by fear, energy lines will contract around the kidneys (water) and adrenal glands, also resulting in a shutting down of our natural life force and enthusiasm.

The fragmented magnetic circuits are like resonating circuits, waiting for outside triggers to give them a chance to move towards healing and resolution. Those resonating circuits have a life of their own that in large part eludes our conscious awareness. They circulate below the surface, so to speak. One job of the cortex is to protect our psyche by keeping the neurons firing internally within the limbic brain (the emotional brain), and thereby prevent overwhelming and life threatening realizations to access our conscious awareness and overwhelm the psyche. It is what psychologists call the subconscious.

You can see these separated magnetic flows as you can see eddies of water in a river. A seer can see them as energy knots. To such awakened persons whose energy is clear, the repressed reverberating circuits are visible because of their density, how they affect our posture, the radiance of our skin, the spark in our eyes, our life vibrancy and general demeanor, how we look, how we speak, how we don't speak – no matter how much we try to hide from ourselves.

Actually, the way we hide things from ourselves (our defense mechanisms) is what reveals them. It is sometimes easier to see those defense mechanisms in others, but usually we don't say anything about it because of the masks of politeness and social conventions (not to be confused with genuine kindness, patience and compassion). At the same time, we tend to have blind spots about our own defenses.

If you see a master, you may be surprised that he may not be just "nice" to you. He may reflect back to you something that you are not willing to see about yourself. Because he comes from a place of unconditional love, he can afford to do so if his motives are pure.

For instance, when I did my first training with Max, I loved the weeklong of teachings and practices. I was my usual self – rather quiet, unnoticeable. Towards the end of the retreat, Max suddenly stopped his expose and looked straight at me. He always has very vibrant, bright and piercing eyes as if constantly tuned to a much deeper level of reality; but this time, it was as if he could see straight through me, as if my whole body was transparent to him.

He said, "you got to speak your truth, otherwise you are going to develop sickness." Then he pointed to my belly and again looked straight through it. He said that such and such artery is stuck under such and such nerve or organ. (I was so awestruck by his energy that I did not retain the technical information, which did not matter anyway because I knew he was speaking truth.)

He added, "When truth comes up for you, it will feel like you want to spit a hairball out. Let it out, speak your truth."

I was fortunate that after the class, he gave me a short treatment of internal organ resetting.

At some point, I could feel the knot softening up and I could tell it was connected to the guilt associated with the loss of my first wife, Jana. This resolved in a big emotional release about not having been able to save her.

Unlocking the Intelligence of the Heart

The secret has always been out in the open. That is the preciousness of your own being, the wish-fulfilling gem, the pearl within your heart. Awakening does not belong to any religion or spiritual tradition. To awaken is to suddenly see who you really are and always were – the most radiant, passionate and alive embodiment of your spiritual essence as experienced deeply within your feeling heart. All paths begin and end at the same place – that is, within your own self. Give yourself permission to shine; who else is going to do it?

Here is something to ponder: if light travels in a vacuum, how does it experience itself if it doesn't have something on which to reflect? Einstein asked himself such a question. Out of relentless desire to know the truth, genius intuition and letting go of old accepted beliefs, he came to the conclusion that from the viewpoint of pure light, the whole universe is a single point and time collapses to zero, with all times being simultaneous.

Of course, the mystics have known this for eons; they experienced it and felt it in the depth of their hearts. As the light of your consciousness shines from your radiant heart, you decide how far it goes and when it coalesces into experience, very much in the same way particles shower into existence inside the vacuum chambers of a particle accelerator. The expanse of your awareness defines the limits of your current reality.

As your heart finds its own answers and reawakens to its unlimited nature, your life transforms; and gradually, your outer reality matches your inner reality.

To navigate the ups and downs that necessarily come with the unfolding of self-discovery, my teachers greatly emphasize the virtues of non-attachment and a childlike playful nature – simplicity, a light and open heart, and living in the moment.

The more you allow and the less you struggle, the easier your life will be. If you're radiating joy, truth, simplicity and love, you know you're on the right track. Keep going and don't let yourself be bogged down by obstacles.

Cherish all lessons, even when their gifts are temporarily hidden from you.

Now, one way to find that secret place within your heart – and I have already stressed its importance – is through stillness. Of course, it is no secret at all, but its simplicity will elude most people until someone or some circumstance inspires them to look for that stillness within.

That is what I practice, or variations of it. After 8 years of practice, I still don't master it. But I have found enough gifts in stillness to know its benefits, both for self and for others.

It doesn't matter to me what you practice, only that you get closer to your goal. The goal is entirely up to you. I can only give you keys that will not lead you on a side path.

Many experiences will come and go. Don't get attached to those temporary experiences and become distracted from your goal.

See the unity in all supreme experiences. Some call them this, some call them that. Don't get distracted by labels. Why would such labels matter when they are all variations of the same radiant truth?

Be the truth, let your heart open, let your heart sing!

My teacher says that if you practice a technique, you will get nowhere. Better, practice the goal! You are bound to attain it.

During the intense grieving period after the passing of Jana, I learned to let go of my linear thinking and really listen to silence to hear her. One technique is called automatic writing, which is equivalent to listening to that small inner voice within. I found that the hallmarks of such "channeled messages" are that they come all at once in a burst of insight (meaning they don't come as sequential thoughts), they are always uplifting, and they always carry a message that is deeply astonishing and revealing (something that the rational mind would not have normally thought of prior to the experience). They tend to result in a shift of perspective and an expansion of consciousness that is somewhat life changing.

One of the very first messages I received from Jana was:

> *There is emptiness, there is grief, there is sadness, hurt and regrets*
>
> *Listen deeper, there is love.*
>
> *Be still, don't run, stay there.*

I have a gift for you.

The gift of your heart, the gift of your soul.

That's how much I love you.

Don't worry about me. I am free; I am happy.

Give yourself permission to be happy,

Pursue your talents; you will have an impact on a lot of people.

Reality Shifts

We see reality as this frozen, immutable space in which things exist in a certain place and events happen at a certain time; and we see ourselves as separate observers of all that.

A little introspection will quickly reveal that inner reality and outer reality cannot be so simplistically separated. Outer reality is vastly conditioned by our inner reality, our mindsets.

When inner vision opens up, it is not so much that outer reality will suddenly look much different. It will stay pretty much the same, although it may become more vibrant, more alive, more "3-D," so to speak. But what may change is your perspective, your overview, your ability to see the connections between things and events. This, in turn, is what allows reality to change and evolve. The more inflexible your mindset, the more dense reality appears to be.

Things appear frozen to us only because, in general, they change so slowly. But observe your reality now. It is not the same as your reality this morning, it is not the same as your reality last week, it is not the same as your reality ten years ago. The reality of this moment will never repeat itself in exactly the same way. You cannot grasp it, you cannot hold it, you cannot catch it, you cannot get it back once it's gone.

In "reality", things are not frozen and they are not disconnected. What may look like an isolated event actually has a life that extends in the space-time continuum.[4]

Reality is constantly evolving. On the other side of the veil (the spirit world), they call it the tenuous world because there, things shift so fast, directly created by your mind. On this side (the physical world), it takes more time for changes of mindset to affect reality. That's what gives us the opportunity to enjoy tangible experiences, to learn and to evolve. Other than that, I believe that it is not that different.

When, through the opening of your inner vision, you see interconnectedness and hidden causes and effects, the same physical world appears under a new light to you. If the change is drastic enough and affects your beliefs, it may feel as if you are opening to a new dimension. In reality there are no dimensions, only a continuum of possible experiences and a new understanding of what you accept to be possible.

Why am I saying all of this?

It is to open you up to new possibilities.

There are so many so-called negative realities in this world – hunger, poverty and homelessness. And people hurt each other in unimaginable ways – violence, crime, wars, conflicts and oppressions of all sort. Even when we enjoy freedom from

---

[4] *To visualize this, imagine that as you move your hand through space, it leaves a "hand-trail." You can visualize the present moment as illuminating one particular position of that hand-trail, like taking a cross-section, a slice of the 4-dimensional space-time.*

oppression and material concerns, we find ways to complain and reasons to be unhappy. All of these are mere symptoms that we have forgotten how to honor ourselves and honor each other.

Usually, people will wait for things to fall apart, for crisis or illness, before they turn inward to make some personal changes for the better.

I have done that plenty of times, and every time I come out of the dark night, I always wonder, "isn't there a faster way, a shortcut through all this suffering?" If the purpose of suffering is to awaken us back to the reality of love, couldn't we wake up before crisis occurs?

I believe we can. It takes only a moment, an inner realization, for reality to shift. Things are never "frozen" in time.

Now don't water the weeds with anger, judgment, fear and despair. Care, yes; feel, yes; but see it all in the light.

Actually, a little introspection will quickly reveal that true courage and strength doesn't mean that you don't have fears; it means that you are willing to face them. You are willing to face your own fears, rather than externalize them. Then you can move in a positive direction – allowing things to return to a natural state, or state of perfection.

When you can hold everything in the image of perfection, you hold within yourself the potential for it all to become that. (You must have heard the saying "what you resist persists." Doesn't resistance create the illusion of physical density, when in truth, we know that matter is mostly empty space?)

The paradox is that to hold the image of perfection within yourself, you don't have to be perfect at it. It can only occur when there is a softening, a surrender within yourself. Striving to be perfect can create rigidity, the opposite of what you were seeking in the first place.

The only reality is Love. When love is blocked, it may create monsters but underneath it is still love.

Life's frailty is apparent in acts of destruction. When I say the only reality is Love, it means that no matter what it looks like on the outside, in this physical reality, there is always a level beyond all illusions and self-deceptions where there is only Love. Love is stronger than death, stronger than time and stronger than any limitations of space. At the level of this physical reality, which you can call the mundane world if you'd like, life must be taken care of and nurtured in order to blossom and show its gifts.

To nurture life is natural and does not require any contrived effort, especially when we are in touch with our true self.

Sri Ramana Maharshi once said, "Your own Self-Realization is the greatest service you can render the world."

This is also the well-known injunction of Socrates: "first know thyself."

Knowing is not merely intellectual. The intellect is only a tiny fraction of your capacities. Indeed, the intellect is a wonderful thing if it is at the service of love and intuitive knowledge, which are far more encompassing and wise in their reach.

Let me give you a simple example. We know that babies need nurturing touch and skin contact from their birth onward. A sensitive mother, in touch with her feelings and life force, will not need any scientific confirmation for that. However, someone who only relies on the intellect will need a scientific study, with control groups and double-blind studies, to establish such things as facts. To such person stuck in the intellect, doubt is the scientific standard.

The scientific method is the science of doubt; love is the science of knowledge.

The great scientists are the ones who infuse their research with true inquiry, trust their deepest convictions and intuitions, and are not afraid to let their intellect be in service to that. They are the ones willing to abandon old conditioning and paradigms. Great discoveries never came through the scientific method, but through the sudden spark of intuitive knowledge. There are many examples of such great discoverers, like Albert Einstein who is best known to the public at large.

I left science behind a long time ago because at some point I came to realize how disconnected I was from my own truth. I wrote a doctoral dissertation – *Measurement of Electronic Cyclotron Emission On the Tokamak Tore-Supra*; it is filled with equations and technical information, but in there you will not find one single line that is me.

After this realization, I could no longer take refuge in equations.

Nowadays, I don't read about science. But interestingly, I have a more direct understanding of nature than when I was doing scholarly studies.

The transient nature of outer reality, as I started to describe at the beginning of this chapter suddenly felt very palpable one morning while I was sitting in our garden with my wife, simply enjoying our morning tea, surrounded by beautiful nature.

We see this world as somewhat flat (actually the 3-D space), in which you could imagine time as a separate "vertical" dimension (the fourth dimension).

In this vision, our present, our "now," is a horizontal cross-section of the 4-D space-time. But this vision is only a narrow, tiny fraction of reality, due to the fact that we are never really moving compared to light. Even if you are in a rocket ship going at 20,000 miles per hour, this is still a negligible fraction of the speed of light, which is 670 million miles per hour.

Now remember, you are light that has been slowed down so that you have time to experience and enjoy this physical reality.

If you could speed up to an appreciable fraction of the speed of light, you would observe, as it has been proven by scientific experiments, a sort of distortion in which time and space contract; not to mention that your body, of course, would start to dematerialize. Also, simultaneity, which we consider as absolute in our mundane experience, would actually appear to be relative.[5]

---

[5] *A lot of the materials in this chapter are derived from Einstein's theory of special relativity and my interpretation of one of my old physics books, Geometry, Relativity and the Fourth Dimension by Rudolf Rucker. The basic question Einstein asked himself was, "If I was riding on a particle of light, a photon, what would the world look like? What would other photons look like? Would they stop moving compared to me? How could I see them then? (In order to "see," that particle/wave of light has to reach your eye.)*

Although I don't intend to write a physics treatise here, it may help you understand this chapter better if I give you a little physics background.

So instead of seeing the universe from this flat perspective I described earlier, we would actually be looking at the universe at an angle, depending upon our speed, in which some intervals of space are converted to intervals of time, and vice versa. This just means that we would be taking a slice of space-time (that cross section I described earlier) at an angle instead of horizontally.

To picture this, imagine a forest of regularly planted trees. The row in front of you appears spacious, but if you look at an angle, the trees appear to be closer to each other. They will even overlap if the angle is great enough. How does this translate to the space-time continuum?

While two separate events appear to be simultaneous for a standing observer, it may look to a different and moving observer as if one event occurred before the other; and their order may even be

---

Einstein's theory is based on the deceptively simple reasoning that if a phenomenon is natural, it should not depend upon the reference frame of observation. Light is a phenomenon of nature (its speed is predicted by the equations of electromagnetism, a description of electric charges' properties and effects), so it should be unchanged upon change of reference frame; that is to say it should be independent of the speed of the observer.

So Einstein concluded that if light is the absolute, then it must be time and space themselves that must be relative. This is a complete shift in paradigm from the old physics in which space and time are absolute and speed is relative to the reference frame of observation.

Now, this theory is called "special" not just because it is so astounding, but because Einstein restricted his reasoning to motion at uniform speed.

Later, he extended his theory to accelerated motion; hence the name General Theory of Relativity. Again it is based on a very simple reasoning that one cannot fundamentally distinguish gravity from accelerated motion, and therefore, they must be of the same nature. He theorized that gravity is indeed a warp in space-time caused by matter, resulting in the acceleration towards center of masses – acceleration we call gravity. Interestingly, one of the sayings of my teacher, Max, is: mind is gravity. This is a powerful riddle, a key, to free our mind from the shackles of illusions and limited perception.

changed depending upon the direction and speed of that observer (this is called the relativity of simultaneity). Therefore, there is no such thing as an absolute present that applies to the whole universe. That means the concept of universe is actually entirely individual if two observers can't even agree on what is past and what is future.

The mind can hardly grasp this because it is so conditioned by our perception in this "slow" moving world, in which those effects are completely unnoticeable. However, I believe it is Einstein himself who said something to the effect of, "if you cannot explain relativity to a 6-year-old, then you haven't understood relativity."

He also said, if you are not in deep awe of the implications of relativity, then you have not understood it either.

Now just so you don't get too fancy on me, this fluidity of simultaneity applies to events that are out of each other's cone of causality.

The cone of causality is the 4-D region of space-time of all the points that can be reached by a beam of light or any slower moving object from a given location in space-time.[6]

---

[6] *To help you visualize this cone, imagine we live nearby, and you read this book 2 years after I wrote it.*

The information has to cover a small horizontal distance (the extra distance to and from the factory is unnecessary for the sake of the argument), but that information has to cover a "large" vertical distance of time. I repeat, time is not really a vertical dimension, but this gives us a practical mental abstraction for visualizing a series of times in one mental picture, or visualizing a 4-dimensional space.

On the other hand, let's say I post an article online and you read it 1,000 miles away from where I live. Now there is only a tiny "distance" of time to cover (the time for the signal to be relayed from the satellite plus the software processing), but the information has travelled a large horizontal distance.

So you see in this physical world, the furthest you can reach in space-time is a region of space included in a cone which angle is determined by the speed of light.

Can you visualize this cone now?

Interestingly, all points of space in my "now" are outside of my cone of causality. To reach those points, information would have to travel instantly, which is faster than the speed of light.

(However, I don't believe that's the end of the story. I believe there is also non-local transfer of information, a fancy way to say that we are all connected beyond space and time. There are no limits to interconnectedness in the great cosmic reality. Einstein predicted that non-locality (today known as the Einstein-Podolsky-Rosen paradox from the names of its co-discoverers) but because he was very uncomfortable with it, he called it "spooky action at a distance," a remnant of the old physics paradigm. But you can refer to recent experiments in modern physics; such as quantum-entanglement, you will see that it gets closer and closer to the views of the mystics. In everyday life, we can experience synchronicities that show that everything is always connected beyond time and space. I have also experienced that if I have a shift in consciousness (for example after a meditation session), that shift will be reflected back by someone I'm closely connected with; and they will show a similar shift in consciousness, even if I don't tell them about the shift I experienced earlier.

But from the viewpoint of a particle of light, to which time has collapsed to zero, all points are "now" and the cone of causality becomes the entire space, one single point of space and time – cause and effect have collapsed into one.

Don't worry if you cannot experience this; you are not meant to, at least not yet.

Remember, as I wrote in the introduction of this book, you would have to transmute your body into light, and there is much you came here to do in physicality before you can return to light.

Those who can travel with the physical body into light are said to be "Dwelling in the Land of the Buddhas" by Buddhist, or "Riding the Celestial Winds" by Taoists, or "Merging with the One without a Second, the One without a Cause"

Your "world-line," which is the 4-D ribbon of your existence in the time-space continuum, must obviously be contained within your cone of causality. It contains your physical existence, as well as all of your experiences and journeys in consciousness. Contemplate the following: where did you start, where are you now, and where are you going?

Interestingly, the origin of your cone of causality is in this present moment. Its true location is not in your head but in your heart. You have a past cone, and you have a future cone. In the image of vertical time I described earlier, the future cone opens up and extends upward. The past cone is reversed so it opens and extends downward.

Another useful and more accurate image, since time isn't really a vertical dimension, is to see time as a sort of implosion-explosion. This is what happens in black holes, by the way.

Actually, think about it, where is the past? Where is the past to be found? You will not find it anywhere but inside you.

Where is the future? Where is the future to be found? Nowhere, but all around you, in the infinite sea of potentials that come into manifestation in this present moment through the power of your choices.

---

by other mystics. For you scholars out there, I don't read scriptures, so please forgive me if this does not match your definitions.

One more paradox is that you already know all of that, and much more. This is why one of my favorite expressions is, remember...

Remember, time is not what you think it is. The part of you that is beyond time has already experienced all of that; this is no joke.

(Now not to confuse you, but I wrote this 2 years ago and my viewpoint has now reversed, as you will see in part 2 of this book. How could two opposing viewpoints be valid at the same time? It is because from the viewpoint of spiritual laws, which are the mirror image of physical laws, things are reversed. The past is found outside, leaving its marks as the present moment. The past has already come into manifestation, yet continually evolves in the present moment, which is the only thing we see with our physical eyes – like seeing the tip of the iceberg if you will. The future is inside us, waiting to be manifested through the seeds of our intentions and actions, as a consequence of this present moment and the infinite potential that it holds.)

If you think that you are not entirely creating this physical reality, it is only because you are not seeing the whole picture. Reality is a co-creation. Everyone has the same power of creation. Also, this present reality is a product of all your past choices, many of which you have forgotten.

So maybe the implosion-explosion is more than an image; but perhaps it is the pattern of creation that we can see throughout the universe.

For example, before living in the tropical jungles of Maui, I never noticed how nature makes the passion fruit. It starts as a bud, which becomes a most beautiful flower that literally looks like a crown. In its center, the pistil has a little ball that further expands and grows into a lilikoi fruit. And it doesn't stop there. Inside the fruit are seeds, encapsulating pure life force inside a protective shell. If the shell breaks out in the right conditions, a new lilikoi plant can grow.

Many traditions connect spiritual awakening with the opening of the pineal gland, also known as the master gland of the human body. They call this the secret square inch because in the ancient traditions, the techniques to awaken it were kept secret. Those techniques were only given to the yogis and monks who proved their dedication and perseverance with years of austerities and preliminary practices for purification. When the pineal gland awakens, it will feel as a flower blooming. You may even experience the dripping of a blissful elixir, sometimes called elixir of immortality from the secret square inch, down your throat and reaching the heart center.

Did you realize that all things in the universe revolve around a center? And that research shows there is a massive black hole at the center of every galaxy?

And have you ever seen photos of a star at the end of its life, in a stage of implosion-explosion with jets of matter and energy projecting upward and downward?

Similarly, isn't this the process of creation in our own lives? Isn't time with you at its center and in your heart, at the center of creation with its infinite unfolding and expansion in both directions, past and future?

So many traditions decry the physical body. Did God make a mistake when he/she created atoms? Did he/she make a mistake when he/she created galaxies? Did he/she make a mistake when he/she created you? Isn't your body at the center of your universe – your vehicle for time travel, for learning, for the exuberant expression of your joy and life force?

Please honor yourself as if you were the most precious thing in the universe, because you are. When you can do that, then you can honor others in the same way.

I believe that the highest siddhi is the siddhi of the physical body. If you did not have a body, you would do everything you could to get one. Your body is your vehicle for evolution. Just observe in your dreams how difficult it is to master your mind. But in your body you have so many tools from which to learn and play.

In the siddhi of the physical body, you take your body with you to the light and past the light, to its source. That's how much love is inside you. You can research this if you want; it is far less uncommon than you might think. My teacher says that in the temples, that's how they see who is enlightened. This one casts a shadow, this one casts a shadow...oh, this one doesn't cast a shadow. (It's probably the one laughing all the time.)

Have you ever seen the Dalai Lama? He is always cheerful and he cares so much. If you ask whether he is bothered by all the people worshipping him, he laughs and says, "I'm just sitting here." (I heard him say that in an interview documentary.)

Now let's get back to our cone of causality. You cannot change causality within your past cone.

But you can experience your life history in an accelerated time frame. For example, at the moment of death, when the mundane mind dissolves and consciousness returns to clear light, or during a near-death experience, you can experience a complete life review (from the all-encompassing eye of Love) in just a few seconds of linear time. Thus the expression "life is short" takes on a whole new meaning.

Note that points that are out of each other's cone of causality are always only an infinitesimal distance apart, no matter how many light years separate them. Remember from the viewpoint of pure light, of pure love, there is no time, space or distance.

We are literally swimming into each other's cones of causality. Although their origins may appear separate, it is not long before the cones intertwine and blend; hence, our shared reality.

What a fun universe, isn't it? If we allow it to be…

What I have experienced is that it is possible to go to the past in consciousness and truly heal it. When the past is healed, you affect the chain of events resulting from it, some of which reside in your past (in consciousness) and some in your future (your potential). The clearing is far reaching. You do that simply through sincerity of feelings in this present moment, until there is nothing but love and compassion. Once the past is cleared through resolution of your feelings, it stops nagging you in the present and you can live life more fully. You can manifest your true potential.

Again, I am saying all of this only to open your mind to new possibilities. The main thing is that you allow yourself to raise your vibration, by whatever means that is (prayer, contemplation, breathing method, chanting, meditation, energy cultivation, movement, stillness, etc.). It doesn't matter how you do it; what matters is that it allows you to be the highest expression of your true nature as love and joy. Then you can radically shift your current set of realities.

When you raise your vibration, you speed up closer to the speed of light. Of course, you are not moving, not going anywhere. What you increase is your spin and your coherence, which is the lining up of your atoms, cells and entire energy system to spin in unison in a consistent direction.

This level of alignment is actually the only difference between a so-called regular person and what you would call a master (whether a spiritual master or a true master of any art or discipline).

Now to take the mysticism out of all this, remember that alignment and one-pointedness of focus are a direct reflection of your intention and the vibrancy and purity of your feelings. When you are in love, you don't worry whether or not you have one-pointed concentration; you just have. You don't worry whether or not all your thoughts and actions line up; they just do. When you are enjoying a good movie, you don't worry whether time passes slowly or quickly. You just enjoy the moment.

Remember that simplicity is a doorway to truth.

Now not to go too Zen on you, but the highest form of concentration is not one-pointed concentration, which is only a doorway; but no concentration at all because that is when you are most open to all that is.

In all his transmissions, my teacher greatly emphasizes emptiness. Emptiness is the key to the universe. If you understand emptiness, you will understand a lot of things.

Remember, you cannot try to be empty; you can only surrender to emptiness.

In true emptiness, there is nothing to empty. You can ask yourself if emptiness is indeed a key or an attainment. I do not master emptiness, but the way I see it is that there is no more separation, only oneness. The ordinary mind merges with its original nature as clear light, unbound by any obstacles, neither in time nor in space.

Maybe I could end this section with a conversation I just heard between my wife and my 4-year-old son as I am writing this chapter. It is close to sunset time and the light is getting low. We just spent a beautiful day at the crystal pools formed by the lava rocks on the westside of our magical island of Maui. We are all super charged by this fun day playing in the sun and the ocean.

Janet:

"It's getting dark here."

Ayden:

"I can still see."

Janet, playfully:

"Well I see you. Can you see me?"

Ayden stops for a moment to ponder the question. As he raises one eyebrow and looks into the distance, he answers confidently and with a smile:

"I only see myself."

The Practice of Giving and Taking

This is a simplified version of the Tibetan practice of Tonglen. It was first written by master Langri Tangpa (1054-1123).

I keep it as simple and easy to apply as possible. If you like the more traditional approach, please find a qualified teacher to transmit the practice to you. You can find very good initiations into this practice in *The Tibetan Book of Living and Dying* by Sogyal Rinpoche and in *Tibetan Book of Yoga* or in *How Yoga Works* by Geshe Michael Roach.

I have experienced such depths of healing with this practice, which is why I love to share it.

With this practice, it is possible to heal past regrets and hurt, send healing at a distance, and have a positive impact on things you would normally consider yourself powerless to improve. You can send healing anywhere in the past, in the present, or in the future.

Remember the simple truth that we are all directly connected and that our thoughts affect each other in a deeper way than we usually acknowledge.

Remember that from the viewpoint of light, there is no space, time or distance. This is true whether you look at it like a mystic, or from a purely scientific perspective.

What allows for immediate synchronized action of your whole being is not just your willpower, nor all the subconscious mechanisms that make your body work.

DNA, the direct manifestation of your energy blueprint, is the building block of your physical body. Scientists have established that your DNA emits particles of light so that your cells can be in constant communication with each other. This also means that we are swimming into each other's field. Just observe how when someone enters into a room, their energy will immediately be read by others who are present, and vice versa, both consciously and subconsciously.

If somebody is having a bad day, sincerely reflect to them how beautiful they are, and you'll immediately see a bright smile coming back on their face. You can see the same results with simply holding positive thoughts towards that person.

Have negative thoughts about someone, and you will have an immediate feedback loop creating a negative experience with that person, confirming your reality. That is how supportive this universe is of your every thought.

By the way, scientists have also established that your DNA is directly affected by your emotions; so as you do your spiritual practices and surrender to your blissful nature, you are actually giving new instructions to your body, which is constantly rebuilding itself.

How does your body know how to build an arm or a heart? It is encoded in your DNA. Your DNA contains the whole history of the human race. This is reflected in the structure of the brain.

The triune brain reflects three levels of consciousness, also a representation of past, present and future. The most ancient part of the brain, the reptilian brain, is in charge of survival and instinctual responses.

The more recent mammalian brain, or limbic brain, is the feeling brain that we share with all mammals. This is why we can connect so easily with cats and dogs, who often come into our lives to teach us about unconditional love.

The cortex, the latest layer in brain evolution, is devoted to thinking. The cortex also exerts some control over what kind of input from the lower levels of consciousness will be allowed to reach your awareness.

Neither the DNA nor the brain are the source of your consciousness; they are simply a reflection. They are your spiritual essence made manifest in this physical world by your own choices. This is why a sudden awakening experience, or sometimes a life-changing event, can completely turn around the way you think and the way you see the world and yourself.

It is also possible to completely heal and rejuvenate the body anytime. How? You simply give your DNA the programs of bliss and joy, the expression of your original nature, instead of the old programs of fear and struggle ingrained by old experiences.

From the way we think, feel and act, to the deepest reach of our light-emitting DNA, it is clear how much we all affect each other.

In the practice of taking and giving, we take upon ourselves the pain of another being and replace it selflessly with a joy-giving gift. If you decide to do this practice, it is important that you see the other as perfect, with their shining true nature within. See their suffering as only a temporary clouding of their light. Do not do this practice out of a false sense of superiority, pity or any selfish motive.

At this point most people go into the old separation paradigm, afraid that the other person's pain will be transferred to them, or that they may catch the person's disease or predicament.

In truth, it is the opposite. The very act of selfless compassion is what burns off the suffering, while selfishness and illusion of separation perpetuate suffering.

When I give this practice to a group, I always have at least one person (and often, many) who comes back a couple hours later or the next day and says, "Wow! I was holding this person in my heart with the practice. I haven't heard from him/her in months; and out of the blue, he/she called me to let me know of this amazing thing happening to him/her, and he/she is so happy."

At this point, resist the temptation to take credit for it, for that would cancel further benefits. Simply rejoice in their happiness. Remember, in truth, you are not changing anyone but yourself – the usual ways you think and your attitude towards others. As you raise your vibration, you make it easier for others to shine their light. The same is true in reverse. We are all equal on this journey.

To do this practice, create a special sacred space where you won't be disturbed for a while.

You may do some prayers, such as connecting with your higher self or an inspiring teacher, master or deity that represents for you a sense of unconditional love and acceptance. It is your connection with a higher power that is beyond space and time. You are activating that higher vibration within yourself. It is the sincerity and vibrancy of your feeling that matters, not the particular belief system that suits your nature and personal inclinations or culture.

Ask to be empowered with success with this practice for the benefit of others. Open yourself up for truly magical and miraculous things to happen, and create a reality where all things are possible.

After prayer, the act of faith requires that you let go of trying hard. Just surrender; relax into the deep knowing that miracles will happen. The universe is already lining up to support your positive efforts.

Take a few deep breaths to let go of the grasping mind and fall deeper within your own center, within your heart. Smile. Generate a sense of lightness, of childlike joy and purity, your own awakened nature.

Visualize a beautiful jewel at your heart. The jewel is nestled in a beautiful fragrant flower – either a rose or a lotus, depending on your preference. The jewel represents the true nature of your heart and the flower represents its awakened, open state.

Now bring to mind a person who you know is in some kind of suffering. Transport yourself to where they are right now. See them in what they are doing at that moment, and really feel what they feel.

Maybe they have physical pain, painful feelings, worries, etc. Sincerely feel that pain as if it was yours. Their pain has gathered as a dark cloud, like a little pool of black ink the size of a coin, in front of their heart. Behind that cloud is the light shining from the jewel in the flower at their heart, representing their awakened state – their original nature as pure joy, love, peace, perfect happiness.

Now really make the commitment that you are going to take their pain upon yourself. Do that with the same selflessness of a mother who would rather suffer than see her child suffer. At the same time, see the love, the sparkling light shining from the jewel in your own heart. It has the awesome power to dissolve any darkness. Keep a nice smile throughout this practice so that you stay in your own awakened vibration.

With your next inhale, draw that cloud of darkness up and out of your person's chest and throat. With each inhale, draw the cloud of darkness closer to you, until it floats in front of you. Prior to your last inhale, renew your commitment to selfless compassion, your willingness to take your person's pain upon yourself. Then inhale the cloud of darkness. When the cloud of darkness reaches the sparkling jewel at your heart, there is an explosion with a bright flash of light. The cloud of darkness dissolves into a puff of white smoke, and then clears. The pain is gone, both from your heart and from your person's heart.

At that point, know that that particular pain is gone forever; it will never come back again. See the light shining from the jewel in the flower at your heart. See your person's heart now clear, with its jewel free to shine the light of its true nature. See your person's mood suddenly lifted up. They don't know why, but it doesn't matter because they are happier and more vibrant.

Next, since you have removed their pain, it is important to replace it with a joy-giving gift.

So now really feel what it is that your person really wants. With your next few breaths, still smiling, send that gift to them through the loving light shining from your heart and through the fragrance of the flower. Let the out-breath leaving your nostrils also carry the gift to them. Again send your gift with complete selflessness. Give them all you've got. If you send joy, really feel joy within yourself and generously give it to them. If you send them the inspiration to give and share their own talents and gifts to make others happy, really give them all of your inspiration (this is called the gift of giving).

In this tradition, we also send the gifts of kindness, patience, wisdom and stillness. With every gift you send, you can mentally say, "dear ..., I send you ..."

When you are done, see the unobstructed stream of light connecting your heart to their heart. Feel the lightness and joy present in both of you.

You can now bring yourself back into your body and release the bond you just created with that person. See the light shining from your heart's true nature, connected with the heart of all sentient beings' true nature, across all dimensions of space and time.

Allow yourself a feeling of appreciation and gratitude for your own efforts and continue with your day.

When every moment becomes an opportunity for shining the light of love and compassion, there is no more separation between life and practice. The heart turns "inside-out." This is simply called living presence.

Self-Love

Self-love is spirituality 101. It is the beginning, but it is also the end because it is self-mastery: when you can identify and merge with the all-pervading love, the aspect of yourself that is without a beginning and without an end.

Self-love is an "of-course-ness" that you are lovable – that it is okay to be yourself; that you have intrinsic value and deserve love not because you earned it, but just because you are. You don't need to be self-conscious; you can be natural and spontaneous. Self-love is simply enjoying who you are, and having a direct sense of self-worth and self-respect.

It doesn't mean everybody will love you. Some will, some may not. But that is not the point. The point is that with self-love, you are comfortable radiating who you are.

People who are comfortable with who they are, are fun to be around because they don't go around trying to change anybody. They have an aura of confidence and they make it easy for others to be themselves because they function from a basic enjoyment and zest for life. They are not seeking approval, nor endlessly trying to please others. By natural extent, they are not judgmental of others.

Children are naturally good at that. Watch them play and get excited about everything.

For most of us, as adults, we think we have self-love until life exposes our doubts and insecurities. If we can see those for what they are – the keys that bring us back to wholeness – we can avoid much of the struggles and drama that we put ourselves and each other through, and make great spiritual progress.

At your core, you are love, which is strong, fun, passionate, creative and wise.

If love is nurtured, it blooms. If it is denied, it will try to push through as sadness, anger, and eventually into symbolic substitutes that will look more and more removed from love. If suppressed, the original energy of love will not simply disappear; it will become thwarted, and even mean, if there is no other outlet.

Everything can be healed with love. I mean *everything*.

When love is denied to us as children, our self-esteem suffers. If a child doesn't receive the basic love, nurturing attention and care from his parents, he needs the love so intensely that he will rather doubt himself than see his parents for who they are – still working out their lessons of self-love.

If it goes on for too long, low self-esteem turns into shame, which is feeling bad about your own needs and wants. And if that goes on, shame turns into guilt, which is a form of self-judgment and rejection of one's self, resulting in judgments about others.

I repeat that at any moment, love is the medicine and it is never too late to start healing with love.

Purification of the heart is the removal of all doubts that obscure its true nature.

Its true nature is love; everybody knows that.

But to really embody that in every moment – to reflect it into every word, every action and every thought – means you know that you are love without the shadow of a doubt.

The spiritual quest is very much the path of purification of the heart.

To doubt is human. Everybody has doubt. You think you don't have doubt until life presents you with a challenge that you cannot solve with your present state of consciousness. You set that up yourself out of self-love because that's what you (your soul) want – to embody the full spectrum of the infinite love that you are inside this human body, this human experience.

This is universal truth. However, your job is still to find its unique expression that wants to flow through you as you.

Unconditional love doesn't mean we're going to love and accept everything. It means we don't put conditions on our love. If you think someone is not unconditionally loving towards you, you may be right; but chances are you are also not giving unconditional love. (That's probably why you are doing this dance together.)

Unconditional love means – besides the obvious feelings of true warmth, caring and acceptance of the person in front of us – that we are not controlling and judgmental. When faced with a challenge or a conflict, we don't go into the old programs of reactivity.

We are willing to acknowledge our mistakes and make amends. We're willing to ask ourselves, "What am I meant to learn from this? What is the most loving response I can have?"

We may not have all the answers, but in that not knowing, in that surrender, maybe a true answer will come to our heart. So instead of reacting from fear, anger or despair, we may actually come up with a response that truly moves everyone towards more love and understanding.

Observe how a master deals with a challenge. Because he knows deep in his heart, beyond any doubt, that the only reality is love, he doesn't waste his energy with impulsive reactivity. He knows better not to make things worse. He watches the play of drama without adding fuel to the fire. He may not have an answer right away, so he will smile and remain still. In that stillness, things are allowed to return to their natural flow. However, a compassionate teacher will not hesitate to use firmness or even anger, if that is what it takes to benefit others, restore justice or save someone from danger; but it is never for selfish reasons.

Gandhi had unshakable faith in non-violence. When things got out of hand with craziness, he did not go around and scream. He surrendered and fasted. And he fasted. And miracles occurred. I am not saying everybody has to be like Gandhi. I just want to emphasize that unconditional love is not for the faint of heart; never take it for granted.

You don't have to be a saint to be the embodiment of the Divine Love that you are. Keep it simple: love what is in front of you. Everything in your life is there for a reason. It doesn't mean just blindly love everything and don't question anything; it means put some loving attention into everything. Melt all obstacles with love.

Serve in love. Serve what is in front of you. You don't have to be perfect. I am not perfect. Your imperfections are your teachers so you can love them too!

Of course, real love does not preclude a healthy sense of boundaries and limits. Quite the contrary! For real love to blossom, it is *essential* that you know what you want and don't want, independently of what others want from you.

Your primary relationship is with yourself. Remember, experiences with others – both positive and negative – are reflections on the surface of your mind, different aspects of the one self that separates into parts in order to learn and experience itself.

In relationships, one partner is usually more fire, and the other more water. This seems to happen by a sort of magnetic attraction because we seek balance.

The job of the water person is to speak up and say what they want rather than just go along. Their job is also to cool the fire of their partner when needed. The job of the fire person is to maintain patience, take time to listen to underlying feelings (both in themselves and in their partner), and help their partner into action when appropriate.

Everyone is moving towards balance – the integration of masculine and feminine and the balance of fire and water.

Your dominant traits are greatly influenced by your birth imprint, which is for most of us our first experience with survival in this world.

For example, if the umbilical cord gets wrapped around the neck or if you're stuck in the birth canal for too long, the fight-or-flight response of your nervous system, the sympathetic nervous system, speeds up your vital signs, heart rate and blood pressure. It does this to galvanize your system for action and get you out of your predicament. That's survival.

If you have to struggle for too long, the body risks running out of oxygen. So now, the parasympathetic portion of your nervous system takes over and shuts everything down to conserve energy.

The reptilian brain, whose job it is to keep you alive, is fully functional at birth and will record the experience that allowed you to succeed.

Were you born fighting, crowning your efforts with success, or shut down and defeated? Were you welcomed in the arms of love or left on your own for too long? (Remember, babies live only in the present moment, they cannot rationalize, so one moment is like an eternity to them. Again, this is perfect design of Mother Nature to optimize our chances for survival.)

Those early imprints of survival will play a large role in how you view the world and how you respond to it in general, but also particularly in challenging and emotionally charged situations. These imprints are not merely psychological; they affect your whole body chemistry during your most sensitive years of development, and will get grooved into the dominant traits of your personality.

Did you know that in the old days, when babies were born with anoxia (blue), they were held upside down by the feet and slapped to be shocked back into life? How do you think this affects the sensitive human being, coming fresh into this planet?

Nowadays, much progress has been made. Many see the benefits of a natural and gentle birth. Hospitals understand the importance of skin-to-skin contact, rather than prolonged and cold separation.

Did you know that it is the baby who decides when it is time to be born? The baby, when ready, will release its own hormone called oxytocin, (sometimes called the love hormone), which signals the mother to start the birthing process. This is very different from a scheduled birth at the doctor's convenience! No wonder why so many feel disempowered in this world.

Did you know that the most common mistake is to cut the umbilical cord too soon, when it is still pulsating with the precious blood and life-giving oxygen? If you wait enough, the pulse naturally dies out; that's when the baby starts breathing and it is time to cut the umbilical cord. Every mother mammal in nature knows that, but only man, with his sophisticated technologies, ignores that.

Now, I'd like to share a personal experience that will illustrate some aspects of dealing with imprints on our survival brain.

This morning I woke up with a pit in my stomach – a sort of dreadful, uneasy feeling and a darkness disproportionate with the present. Rather than fight it, try to change it or ignore it, I decided to embrace it, to go into it without judgment of good or bad. I immediately remembered a scene from my childhood, during my early years at school. I was having a good time, joking and being boisterous with my friends. I must have said something offensive to this older kid; I did not mean to, but I'm sure I must have been insensitive. The sudden look of rage on his face terrified me so much that I jumped out of my chair, ran out of the classroom and into the schoolyard. When he caught up with me, the terror overwhelmed me and I collapsed at his feet, grabbing his leg and screaming "no!" I felt as if I was falling into a black hole, more terrified at my own experience than what was really happening. It was like discovering a huge pit of darkness inside me, and I was changed after that experience. Then by magnetic pull, throughout my school years, I kept attracting those kids who wanted to pick a fight with me. Every time I was so terrified that I turned pale and even got sick at times.

But this morning, as I melted into the experience, it was obvious to see it as a fear of death. As I melted into it, the dreadfulness disappeared and freed this incredible feeling of life force within me. The pit of darkness in the stomach became the life force itself that had been repressed, and yet was pushing all along. Of course, once the fear is felt and truly embraced, it disappears because it has given its gift and that particular lesson has been learned.

Now everything I just described here only took a moment, because remember, in consciousness there is no time.

I must remind you to not misunderstand this by thinking that you have to "try" to heal the past or make yourself "go" into it. That's not how it works. If you do that, you will only create more grooves for yourself and reasons to be unhappy. Your only job is to be present with what you are feeling right now; be love, be joy, and the rest will take care of itself.

As you open yourself to your joy – that light-hearted bubbly feeling in the heart – everything that doesn't match it will come to the surface to be released in its own time, including stuff from your ancestors that has been stored in your DNA.

It is a natural process of letting go and returning to source, to your original nature.

As you surrender to your blissful nature, you give new instructions to your DNA to no longer build your body from the old programs that plagued you before.

Bringing your divine essence back into this human form is what is called bringing Heaven on Earth.

Remember, Heaven and Earth come into balance into your heart.

The merging of Heaven and Earth also means the merging of the ordinary mind with the awakened mind. The mind returns to its unlimited nature, the oneness with the spirit from which it comes. It is the merging of the finite with the infinite.

If I can share from my humble experiences, I believe that there are three stages of awakening. First is the awakening of the energy body; second is the stillness or purification of the mind; and third is the realization of oneness.

Those stages are not sequential, but they blend, intertwine and merge with one another. The highest spiritual practices are non-gradual methods, since all that is required is the spontaneous surrender to one's own true nature.

Remember, it is not the quantity of practice that matters, but the quality, which is the attitude you put into it.

I also believe that self-mastery, the complete alignment with all the different parts of ourselves, is what comes out of a lifetime of dedication to one's own path.

Now I would like to conclude this chapter with something that is worth repeating: it is never too late to start healing with love.

Even when reaching the end of their life, a person can find themselves on their deathbed, humbled, heart wide open. They can still send out love to all those around and be a great blessing to them. They can straighten out their affairs and die happy, in peace and without regrets. (Always forgive those who have hurt you and make amends for your mistakes; that's how you make things right.)

To Love is Divine

To love is Divine,

because to experience Divine love

we are given the gift of loving each other.

Love is the gift of the Divine,

for to feel love is to experience the Divine.

To love oneself

is to experience the Divine within oneself.

The Fruit of Silence

Trust your own feelings, instincts and intuition. They hint at your true nature.

Become your own master, which in time comes with complete surrender.

Be still.

From silence, the voice of the awakened mind can be heard and all choices become crystal clear.

Yesterday at the end of the day, I was listening to beautiful piano music by Franz Liszt – *Harmony Poetiques et Religieuses* – which put me in a heart-melting mood. I lay in bed, next to my sweet family already all cozy and fast asleep.

I'm not doing any spiritual practice, not praying. Just in bliss, melting in positive thoughts…

I empty the thoughts and drink the spaciousness of just being.

The more I empty, the more positive thoughts come back in streams of realizations, flooding me with tears of joy:

There is nothing to get, nothing to pray for,
that is true surrendering.

The mind is not needed to be one with God.
The surrender in silence is the melting in oneness.

What I truly want has no obstacles.
Obstacles are stories created by the mind.

What I truly want is to be a servant to love and joy at
all times.

That is ultimate bliss.

It is not possible to be offended (only the small mind can be).
It is not possible to not love every moment and everyone.
All it takes is the silence that becomes liquid bliss, the space that is
the permanent state inside.

It is then no coincidence that today I come across this poem by
Mother Theresa:

The fruit of Silence is Prayer
The fruit of Prayer is Love
The fruit of Love is Service
The fruit of Service is Silence.

Love and Alchemy

One night I was in pain, feeling disconnected and heavy, waking up from bad dreams. For some reason, I asked to connect to Master Jesus and started to pray and talk to him in meditative state. I asked to be lifted up out of sorrow and into joy.

I suddenly get downloaded with an amazing insight, at the same time that I feel my consciousness expand and get out of its state of contraction.

There is no explanation why, suddenly, this uplifting message came to me and made everything right. The experience was so tangible I could literally feel it flowing in my veins, which is very different from getting it from a book or from someone else.

And as I am feeling the love and the joy expand, and I feel this amazing grace and joy of having Janet by my side, I touch her body and there is a magnetic energy; and we turn around and both crack up laughing.

I did not make any particular noise, but the bliss was so thick that my wife, who I know was sleeping prior to that, could feel it. We shared the bliss as it poured back and forth between us, without the need for any words.

I had heard about the One Law from my teacher before, but this was my first direct experience of it:

"The meaning of death is to free the soul. On the path to awakening, we can realize this freedom while in the physical body. Freedom and love mean the same thing. It is what the universe is made of. It is the One Law, the basic constituent between the molecules of space and time."

Love is the basic and the ultimate alchemy. Isn't it nice that it comes down to something so simple?

Compassion

Conditioning has taught us to separate, divide, defend, protect, judge and label.

Love and Compassion unite.

To be compassionate is to care. To be compassionate in difficult situations is an invitation for us to act from wisdom, not from the old programs of reactivity and survival. These old programs had their wisdom at the time but now they are more likely to compound suffering and drama.

Instead, remember that we are all mirrors of each other.

Love and Compassion dissolve all darkness.

If someone is less fortunate than us, we can take his or her pain away and replace it with light (with pure intention, pure heart). In the end, all we are doing is shedding light on our own darkness and returning to our pristine nature.

Don't just practice that when you feel great and it's easy.

Practice that when it's difficult; it will open your heart like nothing else.

Miracles

I am not a master, so don't expect me to tell you about some big miracles here.

What I would like to talk about are the small miracles – the ones that happen every day and that some people ignore or fail to notice.

I think that many people see those miracles; for them, it is a natural experience. It is a sign that they are connected to their center and they see how the universe lines up to support them.

Miracles are those "wow" moments. In their most simple forms they are signs, synchronicities and amazing manifestations that remind us of a higher level of reality. This physical reality is simply one of its manifestations.

Some miracles happen as an answer to a prayer. Then it is a miracle only to you because you recognize the answer for yourself. Others may not see anything special, while your mind may be blown away at how beautifully your prayer was answered.

If you pause for a moment and stop taking everything for granted, you will see that everything is a miracle.

I did not experience miracles until I delved into spiritual practices. It is what allowed me to really clarify my intention and purpose. Then miracles abound. Some synchronicities will appear so striking that it would be really silly to attribute them to mere random chance and not acknowledge their meaningfulness.

It is one of those funny self-fulfilling realities that the more you open yourself to miracles, the more they happen.

The miracle of life, and my everyday joys with my family, I keep for us to enjoy.

But allow me to recount some simple miracles I've experienced, just for the joy of sharing what a miracle looks like to me. You can recognize how miracles occur for you and learn to trust your own ways.

I will call this one the mosquito incident.

I was going for my morning meditation on the swing in our yard with Ayden, who was a baby at the time. The usual bunch of mosquitoes was swarming around us.

I smile, fully aware that my energy is far greater than theirs, so I decide to surround us with a protective layer of expanding golden light to repel them.

Instantly, not one mosquito around! I was so amazed and amused by this result that I shared it with Janet.

Then, *later that very same day*, I read in my next chapter of *Autobiography of a Yogi* by Paramahansa Yogananda, (the book I was reading at the time) an episode from his years of training with his Guru, titled "how to outwit a mosquito." It ended with the summon from his master: "get rid of mosquito consciousness"; followed by this commentary from Yogananda: "by yogic power, he could prevent them from biting him."

I immediately, of course, felt completely blown-away by the profoundness of this synchronicity and also by the depth of my connection with this book and masters.

Note that I do not particularly care about the "repelling mosquitoes" ability, although it could come in handy on a tropical island. It was just a thing of the moment. I have never done it again since then. Also, there was no way for me to know beforehand that I would be reading about this in the evening, so there is a synchronicity that defies our usual sense of causality.

In this example, which is the cause, which is the effect? It is not possible to answer for sure. But if one sees this as a reflection of a higher guidance at work, then one sees that nothing is impossible. Actually, maybe the only meaning to such synchronicity is to show us that there is guidance at work, or that we are always connected to everything else past all the limitations of time and space.

Another example is my experience with a hernia. A few years ago I was doing some compression breathing combined with an intense yoga-balancing pose – the kind where you dig your elbows under your rib cage to balance your whole body on your arms. This, after eating a full plate of shrimp scampi! (Please don't try this at home, I'm serious.)

Needless to say, you can't get much more silly than that. It sure did not feel good.

After a few weeks of discomfort and acute pain, I went to see a homeopathic/naturopathic doctor. He suspected a hernia. That is when I learned that it is not possible to heal a hernia naturally. The only options are to live with it and minimize discomfort, or to do surgery.

I went to see a Chinese acupuncturist who, to my surprise, said exactly the same thing.

It was difficult for me to hear because I believe all things are possible and I certainly believe in healing miracles.

I decided that I could heal myself. I did not fight the hernia. I simply felt it and listened to what it wanted to teach me. I fasted often and regularly, prayed, drank plenty of water, surrendered, and allowed myself plenty of rest and immobility, lying on my back.

When I did my spiritual practices, I allowed myself to feel it, but I also allowed myself to go into bliss and emptiness without attachment. During practice, I held no judgment of good or bad and no attachment to healing; rather, I just allowed the space to be without obsessing on it. Often, this resulted in all pain subsiding and even disappearing completely. After practice, the pain would be gone and I could sometimes hold that vibration of no hernia for the rest of the day.

I went to see a surgeon. She told me that she was the top specialist of hernias on Maui, and she had no doubt that I had one. I told her my belief that if a certain path takes you to disease, it must be possible to take that path in reverse and heal.

She had a nice smile that seemed to say incredulously "good luck with that." She gave me her card in case of emergency, or for when I would be ready to come for surgery. I thought, great, maybe I can open that doctor's mind to the possibility of miracles.

A year later, after recurring waves of improvement and pain, I finally surrendered. I said, "I've done my best, I don't want to live my life with this constant concern. Now is the time for surgery." However, because the pain was on and off, I wasn't sure whether I still had the hernia or not.

When I went to see my specialist, I asked if we could do some kind of x-ray to see if the hernia was still there. She said she did not need to. Although she could not feel the hernia now, she remembered feeling it a year before and had no doubt about it. She had absolute faith that hernias could not heal naturally. I was scheduled for surgery the coming week.

The night before surgery, my wife read my cards and got that I no longer had a hernia, but that I needed the physical confirmation of looking in there to allow my mind to accept complete healing.

I went in with a cheerful mood, although not sure if they would find a hernia or not. I must say it was a very funny feeling.

Before surgery, I was in a great mood – relaxed and amused at the strangeness of this experience. My pulse was measured at 50! (When I was younger, I did a lot of bicycle riding and my base heart rate then was 60.)

I was lucky I could do a laparoscopy, which is not as invasive as traditional cuts.

Sure enough, there was no more hernia. I have never felt that pain since then. And I got to go home with a beautiful color picture of my guts.

It puzzles me that the surgeon was first 100% sure I had a hernia, followed by being 100% sure I did not have a hernia.

As for me, I'm not attached to miracles. I believe that whatever your mind believes, that is the reality you will create. That is because the universe loves you unconditionally. Remember, you are the universe that flows through you as you. If you doubt, the universe will reflect back to you doubt, until you learn what you had to learn through doubt.

To me the hallmark of a miracle is in its surprising and uplifting effect, not just how big or spectacular it is.

This is an e-mail I just received (of course with perfect timing!) from my friend Donna. I had not heard from Donna in a couple years. She had to leave Maui for the Bay Area due to sensitivity to vog, the emanations from the nearby volcano. Both Janet and I were so moved reading this e-mail that I decided to include it in this chapter without editing it, with Donna's permission:

> "I'll begin by explaining that I have known all along that my life-long "illness" has always been a blessing, constantly pulling me out of the collective reality and back into a stillness so deep that I would merge with Truth. And when my body crashed on Maui and sent me into this lovely cave, I knew that it was a call to a transformation so vast that even my body could express that Truth. We have been descending into a cellular Stillness that allows our cells to become perfect expressions of Divinity and both of us are aware of that upgrade at the very core of our being. I have been beginning every morning by inviting my perfect blueprint to express itself through me. During my 'meditation' I actually watch this blueprint rising up from the empty center (void) of

my cells and radiating outward as perfect health, perfect radiance in every cell. It is important to say that this process is not a 'doing' but rather a surrender into 'allowing.'

It's working!!! Joe was diagnosed with end-stage kidney failure due to exposure to Agent Orange. The renal specialist advised him to begin dialysis immediately but he asked for two weeks to 'invite a miracle.' When the test results came back, he was much better. The doctor was so delighted. She said that she had never seen a recovery like this and that she doesn't even want to see him for a few months.

My own body and reality are transforming. All the medical tests are reflecting wholeness.

Recently I had to go through an electric shock test to test my nerve to muscle conductivity. I've always 'failed' that test spectacularly, which gave me a diagnosis of Congenital Myasthenia. This time, I did my meditation/prayer in the morning before the test and I remembered that there was nothing but Goddess, nothing but joy; that perfect health was inevitable because I was only Love. And so, during the test, as they sent each shock into my body increasing the voltage each time, instead of contracting, I was expanding into Love, into bliss. In that reality there was no illness or weakness or disease to be found and so they have declared me 'healed.'

Of course our minds could not contain this much Truth, but they kept trying. We aren't fully radiant yet but the shock is beginning to fade and what's left is pure joy. Our bodies are catching up with these new instructions. My brain, heart, lungs, kidneys and liver damage have all disappeared instantly. There is still a bit of muscle atrophy from being paralyzed for so many years. And, a couple of spinal discs that were collapsed (because the muscles weren't strong enough to hold them up) are already healing. Literally each day I become stronger and more pain free.

My sense is that our three years here in this cave has allowed us to separate out from consensual reality but that up until now, it was that consensual reality that was physically holding us up. And now we've broken away from that old and very limited system of being but haven't yet plugged into the upgraded form.

I used to teach my students that a caterpillar has to give up all instructions for being a caterpillar. It literally has to turn to soup. Total surrender into no-mind before it can become a butterfly. This has something to do with alchemy. I feel as if I am being transmuted into a different form of matter.

Or could it be that just like I now have to build up my physical muscle strength, that I can't quite hold this new version of myself yet, and so I drop back into the lower vibration that I am so used to forming around? And so I am perfectly well when in that new vibration, and still sick when I fall back into the habit of being the old me. But as I always taught my students, 'We have come to learn to bear the beams of Light.' And I am learning to hold the voltage of this radiant body more and more, but not consistently yet.

After my medical test, we went to a restaurant. We were somewhat in shock (no pun intended). I was saying to Joe that I needed some proof that this was real. As I was speaking, I noticed a homeless man outside the window staring at us. He came inside, put his hand on my shoulder and said, 'I'm hungry. Will you feed me?' I said, 'Of course,' and handed him my pizza. At that moment, the restaurant manager came up and tried to get the man to leave. As he was literally being dragged away, he called out and said, 'I am an angel and God told me to tell you that your love is real.'"

To conclude this chapter, I would like to suggest three simple steps to open yourself to miracles or learn to recognize those already happening in your life.

First, connect to your inner guidance (the name you give to that is up to you). It is a sense of lightness within your heart, of love and wisdom that is beyond the limitations of time and space.

Second, sincerely ask for what you want. Be vulnerable and open. Ask out loud if that helps you. Line up your true desire with your highest, most noble intent. Let yourself be one with your intent; see it as already happened, thereby triggering a sense of joy and contentment within yourself.

Third, in order to receive, you have to surrender, let go. You see, if you have an attitude of grasping, lack or attachment, then that is what the universe will reflect back to you. In this phase, you allow yourself to be still. Empty yourself so that you can receive. You may not know how you will receive, but it is that openness that leaves room for surprises, that leaves room for miracles.

The paradox is that the less attached you are, the more you will manifest. Accept that you may not get what you want. Let it go. Trust that the higher power, the universe, your higher self knows what is best for you and is already lining up to support you.

Maybe you are meant to learn something from not getting what you want just yet. Maybe it's to leave room for something even better to come to you.

Let go. Allow time to work for you.

Let yourself be surprised, open yourself to miracles!

Interestingly, as your power of manifestation increases, you'll want less and less, and you will become more selective about what is really important to you.

You will see that what you want the most are not things at all. You will see that the happiness of others is what's most important, to the point where all sense of separation will dissolve into pure love. This is when the heart turns inside out and the inner world and outer world merge within yourself.

When you open up, you see that there is nothing that you haven't manifested for yourself; and that when you are ready to shed your limitations, the universe is at your fingertips.

Prayer

Reading beautiful stories in a book about the Saint Shree Maa, I felt so inspired and uplifted by her qualities and words of wisdom. My heart felt immediately connected to her radiance, so I prayed and asked for a word of inspiration.

A little later, these words spontaneously flashed in my head:

"Feel the Unifying Principle in your life."

A delightful bliss immediately engulfed me and lingered for a couple days. It inspired me with this little prayer/meditation that I would like to share with you.

Remember, experiences come and go. This is only to inspire you to write your own songs of celebrating the Love and Truth that is within you:

I delight in Divine Absorption

I am Divine Absorption

I feel the Unifying Principle within myself and in my life

I surrender into all experiences as a reflection of the Divine

I invite the miracle of seeing this Divine Knowledge burst forth into the heart of everyone, as their exuberant joy, love, sweetness, compassion and creative force

I plant the seeds for this Divine Love to grow everywhere

All I have to do is surrender into Truth; that is Love, Joy, Peace, and in its purest form, bliss and emptiness beyond form and all limitations of time and space

I continually return to simplicity and surrender all my ego attachments, ambitions, fears, doubts and worries onto the altar of the Divine. As I heal this within me, I heal all.

The Inner Journey, It's Just the Beginning

Spiritual practice is the excuse you give yourself to find this shining place within your being. This place where you can simply and completely be yourself.

For some it may be lighting a candle and some incense, and just gently breathing. For others, it may be spending some time in nature in silence. Sometimes it may be taking a long and relaxing bath, listening to your favorite music and letting your mind take a little break. Or it may be watching a very funny movie that makes you laugh out loud.

Whatever it is, it's a place where you can let go of your worries and so-called limitations, and just be.

Of course, you don't need to do anything to "just be", and to find the joy in that, but most of us have forgotten and don't even know anymore that it is possible.

So as you find a quiet, safe and sacred space where you won't be disturbed for a while, allow yourself to be in a positive state of mind (like noticing that you are doing something really good for yourself). Generate a light, joyful feeling at the heart to bring out your childlike playful nature. Smiling is important, even if it feels a little funny at first. It helps you get in touch with your "awakened mind" as opposed to the busy mind.

Pray if you'd like, and then truly surrender, let go. Allow the bliss of your true nature to arise and let your mind go empty.

You will feel a warm, blissful sensation rising up from your belly. At the same time, as you let go of the grasping mind, you will feel like a coolness and emptiness dripping down towards your heart.

In the Taoist tradition that I learned from Max, this is called the merging of fire and water (bliss and emptiness) within the heart, which is the key to your awakening.

All you need will become clear to you, I promise, because your shining true nature is already there; you do not have to work hard at it or make it up. Actually, the harder you try, the less you will get it. The key here is self-surrender; no effort. This is why smiling and keeping a light feeling in the heart is so helpful.

Most people are stuck waiting for something on the outside to change so that they can be happy. But in doing so, you declare that you have no power. You accept a kind of passivity with your life, believing that things happen at random for no reason and that if you're lucky, things will get better. If you are not passive, you struggle and in the process you often make the problems denser.

But you can turn this around, and the paradox is that it is by going within.

When you shine your light from within, then you become the creator of your life.

Then you can sing like the mystic poet Hafiz, "I dance before I have a reason."

Now to me, there is nothing mystical about shining your light from within. It is the very essence of life.

Take the time to really trust your own process and to appreciate yourself. Listen to yourself rather than follow somebody else's truth. Everything you need is within you, literally. This has been said a thousand times, but it is worth repeating.

Take only what inspires you here to remember your own beauty, and ignore the rest.

Laughter really is the best medicine. Be playful like a child. This is what it means to be open, as opposed to all serious and too much "in the head." Things are easier when I can keep a good sense of humor, and they are really a drag when I'm too serious.

Always trust your own feelings, instincts and intuitions; they hint at your true nature.

Cultivate your natural devotion (pure love) and self-surrender.

Keep an open mind; be curious like a discoverer (beginner's mind), and be willing to empty your cup.

Have the courage and strength of your convictions without becoming obtuse or intolerant.

Allow vulnerability. Crying is nature's way of releasing impurities stored up in cellular memories.

Whatever you do, have dedication. Cultivate the purity of your intentions. Focus on your goal with sincerity and vibrant feelings.

Perseverance means not giving up as the going gets rough, or with the first signs of setback. Be consistent in your efforts. But don't be obsessive either. Admit your mistakes and be willing to correct them. Everybody makes mistakes; that's how we learn. So don't beat yourself up; be kind and patient with yourself.

Take regular breaks from spiritual practice to allow your body to integrate. Take time to enjoy life and have fun.

Sometimes, you will go through some major energy upgrades and you will feel zapped. It is time to rest, let your body rebuild, and adjust to the new energies. Listen to your body and what it is trying to tell you.

After spiritual practices, it is important to stay grounded so that you don't go too "airy-fairy." Go outside and hug a tree. Believe it or not, scientific studies show that tree hugging is good for you. If you approach them respectfully, trees can take away your negativities and recharge you with positive energy.

Always seek balance. Keep your focus on life, and don't get sidetracked with side effects of spiritual practices. Anything that comes up in spiritual practice is a side effect. The only measure of positive change is living a fulfilled life, living the life that you want. In other words don't confuse the key (whatever spiritual practice you do) with the goal (the purpose of that key).

Don't take yourself too seriously. Lighten up! If I can do it, so can you! Find the joy in everything; that will make the learning easier!

Be willing to face yourself.

Whatever your practice is, there will come a time when you will have to face yourself. First you see the light of your true nature (or at least, you think you do). Then your shadows come up. At this point, many give up, or start hopping from practice to practice and teacher to teacher, or they want to blame someone or circumstances for their bad feelings. However, this is the most important time to keep looking within and emptying your cup. When opening to more light, everything that doesn't match it will come to the surface to be released. This is the dying of the old ways that no longer serve you, sometimes called the dark night in the forest. It is the deconstruction of the defenses that kept you separate from your true nature. If you research it, you will see that it is a process every spiritual master went through. This deconstruction is what allows the "true you" to emerge. Although you may feel worse during this time, have faith that you are moving in the right direction.

(Sometimes, I feel like an onion with layers that keep peeling off. Although at times it hurts, being closer to Truth always ends up being a sweet balm for the heart.)

Resist trying to rebuild the old defense mechanisms that no longer work, and don't give up. Have infinite patience and know that the dark night is a positive sign on your path to self-awakening. You will learn much from it and it will pass.

Reflect on what you really want in your life and create the conditions to make it manifest. Being tested is a sure indicator that the true light is not far. You will see that every single bad feeling comes down to you not loving yourself. Once you admit that and relearn to love yourself, the universe will open up to you, I promise.

Actually, you can effect this transformation right now. Close your eyes for a moment. Bring your mind into your belly, behind your belly button, and follow the rise and fall of your breath. Now drop the mind altogether and simply feel…

What if you accepted how you feel right now to be the most exquisite thing you could ever experience? All you have to do is open up to that possibility and be without judgment. You see there is nothing to change.

In that simplicity, allowing what you are feeling in the moment to be the summit of your being is a form of self-love. This exquisite experience of the present moment is the most simple form of liberation.

Maybe you can hold this state for half a second, maybe a few minutes. Soon enough, it will be for an hour, a day or a week. Eventually you will walk as a liberated person.

Now remember, with spiritual practices will come changes in your life.

Some conflicts that may have gone unnoticed before will come to the surface.

Whether you like it or not, changes will occur.

At this point, it is important to uphold the highest virtues that you have uncovered through your own efforts.

The universe, in its infinite ingenuity (that's you!), will present you with a test for every realization that comes to you. This is to give you a chance to practice, so to speak, to see how much of your beliefs you truly embody.

I have experienced that deep realizations are often immediately followed by one big test.

If you pass the test, it gets easier and easier. If you don't, you'll fight and moan and repeat the lesson until you get it; it is that simple.

In the old days, this was called initiation.

In the ancient traditions, you had to go to the temples, retreat up a mountain, isolate yourself in a cave, or wander the desert to receive initiation.

Nowadays, there is such a rapid movement towards global awakening that everybody gets their initiation through life.

I love to see how everybody is awakening left and right; it's really beautiful to see. In this accelerated era of information, awakening is no longer reserved to a few selected monks or yogis, but is expressed in all kinds of people in all walks of life. To be awakened has nothing to do with how spiritual you are, but all to do with how passionately you live your life, share your gifts, and inspire and uplift others by mere virtue of your presence.

In my view, the most important virtues are love, compassion, joy, authenticity and simplicity.

Embodying those virtues in thoughts, words and actions is living your path.

Start with contentment and happiness in the present moment. Appreciate what you have and be generous. Stop grasping for more. If you are in a difficult or painful situation, never give up. Have faith that things can improve. Everything is subject to change.

Practice non-attachment. Experiences come and go. Every day is a new day. Constantly empty yourself to become free of mind traps and limitations. Most people confuse non-attachment for a careless and unkind attitude. Actually, the highest form of non-attachment is selfless unconditional love. With non-attachment, we simply free ourselves in the present moment, rather than try to control outcomes with expectations and all sorts of manipulations.

About non-judgment, Taoists have a saying: "Everyone should sweep the snow from his own door and not be concerned about the frost on another's roof."

Be compassionate with all, especially with those who need it most – those facing illness, poverty, and challenges of all kinds.

True humility is seeing the divine in everyone. Never see yourself as superior, nor inferior, for it is just a trap of the ego. Always see the light in everyone, not based on personal preferences but on radiant truth.

Decide what vibration you want to put out to the world. Strive to radiate true joy, liveliness and appreciation for life.

Spend some time every day doing something fun, something that you really enjoy. Actually, the essence of *all* activities should be fun; otherwise, why are you doing them?

Take time to do nothing, contemplate nature and just breathe for a while. In our society which is so task oriented, it is easy to get caught in the doing-doing mode, but that can easily become a form of running away from yourself.

Also, there cannot be true spirituality without kindness, simplicity, honesty and speaking your truth.

To speak your truth is to communicate what's really going on inside, and with a feeling tone. No hiding, no pretense. Share the gift of you. The beautiful Saint Shree Maa puts it simply: "Say what you mean, and do what you say."

Notice the law of balance in your life. A virtue (which here means strength of character), if not applied at the right time and in the right circumstance, can be useless or even turn into its opposite. For example, there is a time to speak up and a time to stay silent, a time to be firm and a time to be flexible, a time to attack and a time to retreat, a time to persist and a time to let go.

The choices offered to us in each moment are what we call free will.

Virtues are not a code of moral conduct, but simply keys to our heart based on the one law of sympathetic resonance between all things. Virtues are the true empowerment of the human heart that remembers its divine origin.

Regardless of the path you have chosen in this life, know that you will succeed because the wish-fulfilling gem is nestled within your heart.

The time is now, why wait?

Who we really are is what's left after we've let go of all that doesn't matter.

The truth is in the heart; let go of the head with all its complications, petty worries, attachments, illusions, distortions and dramas.

Not easy sometimes. Practice.

Practice emptying your cup. Every time you feel the nectar of bliss, empty some more until love radiates in all directions.

Until there is nothing that stands in the way of perfection.

Try it; things will come up – that's purification.

Practice letting go and melting in the heart;
it is not complicated, really.

Even all those words are superfluous. Enter the space of non-duality, the formless, the divine.

There will be highs and there will be lows.

Allow your magnificence to shine when high,

Let yourself be vulnerable when low.

There is infinite beauty in both.

Then you can be magnificent and vulnerable at all times, and that is being authentic.

Embrace all your brothers and sisters, regardless of beliefs and apparent differences.

Love each other and show them that you love them.

We are all on the path of reintegrating our unlimited nature.

The paradox is that we never left it.

The truth reveals itself in glimpses, and little by little we remember who we really are.

The Inner Journey
Part 2   Going Deeper

Preface

As of today, having separated from my wife, I have been propelled on a new phase of my journey (hence, part 2 of this book), mostly through her blessings.

After our magical encounter, joyful years together, and the incredible blessing of raising our children, she must have felt at some point in our relationship that I wasn't always fully there – going in and out of depression, not shining my full self, the self that she was longing for, the wholeness of my love.

Of course, I was not conscious of all that; and our healing journey took me to a place where I could no longer resolve my conflicting emotions.

I now see Janet as the Divine Goddess, whose exquisite sensitivity, truth and love pushed me to go deeper on this journey of integrating my true self.

She encouraged me to go on a cave retreat and bridge the remaining gaps between my words and my day-to-day attitudes.

I have been tremendously blessed. Although the transition was extremely painful and scary, I was also secretly craving that cave retreat.

I am blessed with her continuous love and encouragement; it sometimes blows my mind. We are so lucky to experience mutual support in this co-parenting experience. I see so many leave relationships bitter and ungrateful, bickering and fighting and making their children suffer.

But more than that, I feel that our spiritual connection has grown deeper. She continually blesses me with a deepening on this journey of the fulfillment of our soul's true purpose.

I hope you will see in this second part, that although my essential message is the same, I have chosen to bring it with a more personal tone and more vulnerability.

Introduction

Why do I write?

First and foremost, I really enjoy being creative in this way.

I don't make myself write. I don't ponder, what shall I write about today, or how shall I say that?

Not at all. I empty my cup and things come up on their own, when they want to. I could not make them, even if I wanted to.

To preserve authenticity and spontaneity of the moment, I do very little editing (only for basic flow and grammar).

Any writing is only a snapshot anyway. Not rewriting saves me from headaches and complications.

However, I do write over and over about the things that are close to my heart, and that is my way of refining my expression.

So what is this second part about? Well, you guessed it – the inner journey – the "pathless path" (an expression I learned from my beloved teacher Donna) that everyone must discover for themselves.

"Pathless," because at some point you have to stop following and make your own path if you really want to embody truth – the truth that you are. Eventually, nobody can tell you what is right for you. Not even the Buddha, not even Jesus. Even they, would point you to look at the truth within yourself.

"Pathless," because there is nowhere to go. You know the saying, "no matter where you go, there you are."

"Pathless," because the ending is the beginning, always bringing you back to yourself, bringing you back home.

Finally, "pathless," because there is no path clearly laid out in front of you. (Although isn't it nice when it seems that way?) The path is more like an open sky and isn't this more spectacular?

Usually, we think of outer reality as something we have to put up with or manipulate. Only when things no longer work will most people start to look within and take responsibility for the outer reality they experience.

This is actually not a bad thing; it is a natural process of human evolution and returning to source.

First, we come in as perfect; it is already in our nature to be whole. Then we encounter various circumstances, both positive and negative, and we start learning about the outer world as soon as we take our first breath.

As humans, it is natural and universal (meaning, it is spontaneous and effortless as it is encoded in our DNA) to learn, play and create as an expression of our inner nature and in relation to the world around us. All stages have their joys, discoveries and ways of expression.

This is why I think teaching children meditation is a non-sense. Children are naturally in touch with their inner world, and they naturally express it if they are not repressed or oppressed. If you want to help children, teach adults how to meditate.

As we grow into adulthood, we see the world through the various necessary filters that are not only appropriate but also essential for our stages of human development. For instance, we experience needs, drives and attractions that are wired into our very nature and push us to connect and merge with other souls. These filters also reflect, to some extent, acquired conditioning due to both positive and negative attributes picked up from parents, friends, school, society and culture.

Then as life experiences accumulate, and we understand that there is only so much fulfillment the outer world can give us, we are naturally drawn to return to wholeness. Our task becomes merging the two: the inner and outer worlds. Some find this merging, this union, with a partner, and some find it alone. Many are stuck thinking it has to be one way or the other. My best advice is, be happy where you are. If you trust life, it will always take you where you need to be. Remember, every path is sacred.

When the time is right (it comes naturally, there is no need to force anything), everyone can find for themselves that sacred place within their heart that opens things up for them and allows them to realize that union, the merging of dualities. I respect and appreciate all ways because I can see their common roots.

As I already said in the first part, what gave me access to depths of opening is the KUNLUN® Method (path of no more learning) and for this, I am more grateful to Max Christensen than any words can convey. It continually blows my mind that I was so lucky to meet such an experienced and generous master. He has given me the keys that I had been longing for my whole life. In the old days, masters were so preoccupied with maintaining purity of teachings that they were very spare in sharing them. It takes enormous courage to open up those teachings to everyone like Max did.

What I am sharing in this book could be considered the end result of my personal practice, and the various keys that come to me as I go through my journey.

I share because nothing lights me up more than sharing.

The only reality is love. It is possible to merge with that reality, to see it as tangibly as you see objects around you (actually even much more tangibly).

At the moment of death, when the conceptual mind dissolves, the great mystery unveils itself (or at least part of it) and only love and oneness remains. People who work with dying patients can attest, and so can people who have lost loved ones. Many verifiable accounts of near-death experience (NDE) and even after-death communication (ADC) can attest.

Of course, it is not necessary to wait until the moment of death to open up and appreciate the gift of life.

The highest spiritual practices have as a goal reaching the body of light while in the physical body. In the KUNLUN tradition I learned from Max, this is called Golden Dragon Body. I have seen manifestations of it. Those things are no longer kept secret and reserved for only a handful of practitioners. Other traditions and other names exist for the transmutation of matter into light and back into matter; for instance, the Body of Grace in Tamil literature, or the Rainbow Body of the Tibetans.

I can say all this because I have not reached such stage. I cannot transmute my body into light.

This is a great blessing to me. I don't have to claim anything. Neither do I write to gain anything, so I have nothing to lose. There is only so much time left I do not wish to waste any of it not speaking my truth.

My only message is to share my vision that the only reality is love, that suffering is not the root of human nature, and that it is possible to be completely free of conditioning while in this physical body.

The Spiritual Quest 2

In my years of meditation, which is not much I will confess, I have not found a Self yet, but only Love.

What I mean is that the fulfillment of the self can only be found in loving.

Well, that puts an end to this mad quest.

The Wish-Fulfilling Gem

Sometimes when we are high, we are spiritually low, full of endearing arrogance and delusions.

Sometimes when we are low, we are spiritually high because we are ready to surrender, full of tenderness and compassion.

Either time, I give myself the gift of stillness.

Because we are one, I dedicate my benefits to all.

Stillness is the miracle elixir,
The boon of perfect bliss,
The light of insight.

I'm not asking you to be still for hours; far from that.

I am only making an offering

For you to be radiantly alive, to be yourself

The Self that you, yourself designed a long time ago.

It does not matter if you are more awake than I am;
You can still benefit.

First be yourself, present with your true feelings.

No need to reach for complicated stuff.

No need to reach for unattainable stuff. Everything is here right now.

Let go of all struggles, even if for a moment; return to the simplicity of this moment.

The paradox is that when you do that, everything that your heart desires reveals itself as fulfilled in the present, and the heart is inundated with blissful radiance.

This is why this tender place in the heart is called the wish-fulfilling gem.

Stillness

Be still.

In the stillness is the light,
The perfect bliss, the sweet elixir.

But if I say that, you may start looking for something,
Waiting for something to happen, and in doing so you prevent it.

What a delightful paradox.
Be still, do nothing.

When the words stop and emptiness begins,
The miracle happens.

Because it happens in nothingness, I cannot put it into words.

It is the most simple instruction and yet the most vast and the most profound.

It takes nothing to practice – no preliminaries, no years of austerities, no hidden secrets.

It is so simple that it will pass by most people; but those who taste it know it is the endless reservoir of realizations.

*P*earls of Light

You are a point of light (the visible part) or a black hole (the unseen part) between past and future.

Your consciousness is sitting on the edge of the event horizon. Inside the black hole is the future, what is waiting to come into manifestation.

Outside the black hole is the past, what has already come into manifestation.

Neither past nor future exist. There is only the eternal moment continually unfolding at the speed of light, and that we freeze into form for the sake of our enjoyment.

In the present moment, there is only undifferentiated oneness. Most people are not ready for it because it is more bliss, more voltage than their bodies, nervous systems and psyches can handle.

But we get glimpses every now and then, each time bringing back pearls of light that we can use in our lives.

Shortcuts to Awakening

Embrace philosophies that support life. Leave everything else behind.

The only shortcut to self-realization that I know (which is not much, I will confess) is to embrace life fully, passionately and with purpose.

Dive deep. You will get a few bruises and a few scars. So what? Nobody gains much by playing it safe.

Take the risk to be outrageously alive, in love with existence, no matter your circumstances.

Indeed, your very circumstances are the cocoon inviting you to spread your wings.

Most separate divine and earthly, body and spirit. But how could they be separate? How could that hold together?

So yes! Your circumstances are the cocoon of the Divine birthing itself into existence through you, my dear. (From where else would you start, really?)

Yes, there is non-duality; yes, there is only love; yes, highs and lows can merge at the heart melting in complete surrender; yes, time is only a spec hanging on the surface of reality. But none of this should be of your concern.

These are just side effects of embracing life fully, of loving everything that comes your way – especially what you resist. For what you resist is a gift of the universe inviting you to love more.

Love and accept yourself completely, unconditionally. Even those parts you don't even know are still waiting in the dark, like a lost child longing its way home for a warm embrace.

Forgetting

The shortcut to awakening is not to remember. Stop trying so hard, stop focusing so hard, and stop trying to be what you are not.

Instead, forget! Be completely forgetful so you can drop all your dead-seriousness and self-consciousness.

Laugh so hard that your belly aches. Play, create, sing, paint, dance...forget yourself.

Make no assumption as to where you are. Make no assumption as to where anybody is.

Just be and let be.

Your love is divine, your pain is divine, your oneness is divine, your separateness is divine.

I promise you what's left when you forget yourself is you, which is absolutely in tune with the divine, always has been and always will be.

Spiritual Emergency

At some point, your world becomes too small for you – maybe because of illness, because of life or spiritual crisis, or because of loss. So you want to break the door open.

After you open the door, you have to stop trying to open it again and again. Step into what's on the other side without looking back for safety.

Leave the familiar behind; leave the old world behind.

Don't worry; there is nowhere to go.

This is only an image.

But you will have to shed those thought patterns that no longer serve the higher version of you.

So remember, next time the universe kicks your a**, it's because it loves you so much and knows when you're ready to let go and grow.

Self-Inquiry and Objective Reality

In Quantum Mechanics, the observer and what's being observed cannot be separated but are deeply, existentially interdependent.

Everything is connected to everything else in the great cosmic web of life.

Just the same, you cannot separate yourself from what you are observing.

You are both the observer and the observed and the very act of self-inquiry immediately changes you.

There is no such thing as objective observation. If there was, it would be disconnected, cold and dead – in very contradiction to the warmth of the flow of life, the cosmic dance, the fractal of your beingness constantly birthing itself into new existence.

This is why any meditation method works.

A guru knows that, so he can tell you anything – such as stand on one foot, or repeat this mantra and do not come back to me until you have your awakening.

Many use this to gain power over others.

This is why the true teachers say: don't give your power away, only follow yourself, follow your truth, speak your truth, be the truth.

What Do You See?

Does an eye see an iris, or the beautiful landscape that unfolds in front of it?

You are the whole universe that looks from the center towards the outside; and by some sort of cosmic paradox, you ask, who am I?

The sages will tell you. Shift your perspective.

This is literal.

Flip it around 180 degrees. Looking within, you become whole again.

When the outer world becomes the inner world, you no longer take so seriously all the games of the small self. (But still love all of it because you would not function without it.)

You regain your freedom as a child of the universe.

Then you can embrace it all and dance, my dear. Dance on the altar of your life.

Yes, your life is the offering to the Divine from which you were never, ever separated (not even for a moment).

I have dedicated my life to make this offering to you.

If you think those are mere words, then do this experiment:[7]

Sit in silence, and turn your attention inward.

Really take the time to look within.

You may see images and reflections of the outer world, or thoughts running on the periphery of your being.

Some may not see anything or feel anything at first.

It's okay. Don't be hard on yourself.

Countless practitioners have spent lifetime after lifetime only to gain a glimpse of radiance.

But you don't have to wait my dear. I give you this secret key, which is also the most simple:

Look at that which is deepest within yourself. If you are still on the surface, you can go deeper.

If any thought remains, you can go deeper.

Go to that innermost, most exquisite center, in that emptiness and void – the inner chamber of your heart.

---

[7] *Remember there is no "trying." There is only "do" or "do not." "Trying" means that in your mind, you are already committed to not giving it 100% of your effort. When people tell me they will try something, I already know that they will give up shortly and only get mediocre results.*

It is so bright, so blissful that when you touch it, you will immediately want to jump out of your chair or meditation cushion to run and sing your joy to the world.

And you are right back at the beginning. Only now you see that everything dances on the surface of your mind and the doors of your perception open.

People will tell you that you are a fool.

That's a good sign my dear.

A sign that you are ready to go deeper and that you are ready to start your meditation.

...

After I posted this article online, I received the following comment:

> Wow! I have been so shallow. Deeply, I must allow myself to delve into my existence. Thanks!
>
> My reply: Dearest, don't say that. We are all students in the school of life. Wherever we think we are, there is always a next step. You are fine, always have been, always will be!
>
> Sir, I appreciate you. And where you are in spiritual awareness of self and your divinity. Someday I too shall be. You are a Master, always teaching. Thank you.
>
> My reply: Thank you my dear. My children do not think of me as a master, why should you? Please think of me as a servant. The only reason I post is that day after day, highs

and lows, glorious and not so glorious, I sit down and meditate. It's really no big deal at all, anybody can do it. Anybody that does what he or she really loves will do it day after day; then you can accomplish anything you want.

The Gift

Every experience manifested within and reflected back in our outer reality has a gift.

Usually, we say, "no, I don't want this, I'm not this, I'm not that." And we miss another opportunity to be free.

But that's okay! The universe in its infinite ingenuity will keep knocking at our door, a little louder each time.

The Veils of the Mind

Of all the veils of the mind, judgment is the most insidious and the most rampant.

Notice when you judge someone. Does it light you up or dim you down? Does it empower you or trap you in conflicts?

When judgment comes up (it always does), say, "no thank you, I'd rather be happy." Use discernment instead.

If a behavior bothers you, again, say, "no thank you" and show the ways of love and lightness; it works wonders. Maybe someone forgot something that you remember about love so show them with genuine care.

We all forget. When you forget, would you rather be judged and scolded, like when you were a child? Or would you rather be embraced so you can let go of your worries and remember who you are?

Free yourself from judgment, lighten your burden, everyone will be better for it.

The sages call this letting go of the dross but keeping the pearl.

The pearl is pure love. Pure love is not detached; it is just devoid of ulterior motive or manipulations. Pure love is not removed; it is exquisitely sensitive.

Pure love only seeks to give.

Because pure love is one with its object, pure love is oneness.

*O*de to Silence

Silence is the remedy for judgments and self-doubts; Silence dispels clinging to acquired illusions, yet it strengthens faith.

Silence is the elixir of bliss, the boon of perfect realization.

Silence is pure love,

Silence is perfect compassion.

Yet, most people run away from silence (I have for many years and still do most of the time). One common way to run away is "staying busy" and another common way is to follow dogma.

When you slow down, first you have to face your own thoughts, your own feelings, your own fears and doubts, your own desires and aspirations.

And then you must have the courage to let them refine in the alchemical cauldron (that is nothing but silence itself).

It is not necessary to spend hours in silence. Don't use spiritual practice as another way to escape living your life. Live radiantly;

express your talents, joy and creativity, your unique gifts that are only yours to give.

I suggest seven minutes of stillness because I know it's a safe way to open up.

Many are impatient and want a fast route – they will do drugs, or practice excessive forceful breathing. Then, when they have their openings and don't know how to bring things into balance, or don't understand their symptoms, they start to run left and right, from teacher to teacher for help closing the gates.

The beauty of silence is that it's available freely. You don't have to give away your power and follow anybody else.

And there is more than one way to it.

Each must find his or her own way – the way to the heart.

Although simple, I know this path is not for the faint of heart.

You will be tested; blocks will show up to see how committed you are to your path.

If you are committed to emptiness, you must surrender your blocks to emptiness,

If you are committed to pure love, you must surrender your blocks to pure love,

If you are committed to selfless service in action, you must surrender your blocks to selfless service in action.

Know that there are no obstacles to your realization, unless you want to continue making excuses.

In the space of silence, you become one with all those who have entered that state before you, and their gifts are now yours to give.

It does not matter to what religion or non-religion they belonged or did not belong. The greatest saints will say, leave all of it behind and be willing to stand naked in the light.

Return to source and drink the space of silence. Let the perfect elixir flood down your body.

In the space of silence, *Om Na Ma Si Va Ya* spontaneously reveals itself as a point of light, not a mantra.

In the space of silence, *Om Mani Padme Hum* reveals itself as a blooming of the heart, not a recitation.

Anger 1

There is nothing wrong with anger. Something is calling out to get our attention. It is part of our natural guidance system.

Healthy anger serves justice, integrity and healthy boundaries. It is also simply a way to bring us back to self nurturing after we allow ourselves to get too out of balance.

You can thank your anger. It has helped you survive, maintain your integrity when you were under threat, protected your truth when it was disrespected, and also kept you safe when it was needed.

Anger also served to protect you from deeper demons – fear and terror. Now that you are stronger and in charge of your own life, regaining wholeness and self-love requires you to face and embrace your anger as well as your fears.

Damages come from repressed, displaced or symbolized anger.

(Note that everything I say in this chapter applies to fear as well.)

Underneath anger is the need to be loved, respected and appreciated. Underneath the need to be loved is the need to love, to express our true nature, radiant with joy, playfulness, spontaneity and creativity – that sense of freedom of being our true self.

When angry, we usually focus on what we don't want, giving energy to the very thing we're trying to push away.

So instead, focus on what you want! Express it, not just in words (often words will just create blocks) but also in attitude and with feelings. Then you will notice an immediate softening within yourself because you have made room for what you want.

You will see situations transform; you will see people change. Like I always say, SHIFT happens!

It may not always look like you expected. This is where the expression "Holy shift!" comes from.

Yes, miracles do happen! And if they don't, it's just another opportunity for you to look within and see which part of you has not softened up yet, which part is still invested in maintaining the struggle. But hey, don't dwell on that! Remember focus on what you want, I mean that.

Anger 2

Sometimes a good old fight is what helps release pent-up energies and accumulated tensions. You finally dare to say what you have been holding back, without sugar coating it or putting up a pretense of niceness.

(Please don't confuse this with unhealthy dumping of anger or violence – you must know that any form of verbal or physical abuse is a sign of weakness of character and underlying distress, and should never be tolerated.)

Much opportunity for resolution can follow, as well as reconnecting on a deeper and more authentic level.

This is different from anger delivered with harmful intent.

We all can see how much suffering in the world is caused by rage, hatred, violence, disrespect, symbolized feelings that are projected mercilessly unto others and unto oneself too.

In my experience, all feelings, if followed back to their source, lead to love.

Return to the source of anger – the true cause, the root – you will always find the need for love and the need to express who we really are freely.

Seething anger that is not addressed, resolved and let go will become like a veil separating us from our true nature. If unattended for too long, it is literally a time bomb waiting to explode.

Anger externalized onto the outside world will continue to reflect as negative experiences mirroring our inner state.

Anger that is embraced and honored will lead us back to love, because that's all there is.

As you know, anger is stress-induced. So instead of putting fuel on the fire, it's always good to step back, take time-out if you can! Listen to relaxing music, spend some time in nature, chill and let go of worries; even if it's just for a moment.

Your perspective can more easily shift when the mind is clear and not clouded with anger and frustration. A clear mind will give you better ability to see positive solutions to the problem in front of you.

Being neither a master of anger or non-anger, I would love to end with this beautiful quote from the great mystic Ramakrishna:

> "The seeming anger of a compassionate person is no more than a mark made on water. It vanishes as soon as it's made."

*W*aking up from the Dream 1

I keep waking up from the dream;

Please forgive my improvisations.

I think I am awake until the next time I wake up.

It goes on and on, layer after layer.

So is my experience of the return to simplicity and truth.

When I see a glimpse of radiance, I run to sing it to the world!

What a fool, when I hardly know how to give it.

I should listen to the masters who constantly try to bless me even though I hardly listen:

Don't try to give the radiance, just be it.

Waking up from the Dream 2

Life is what happens when you drop all of your elaborate plans.

Oh, beautiful child of the universe…do you think you can contain that much wildness in a carefully laid out plan of action?

Everybody talks about being in the moment, but when do you take the time to take in the beauty of a flower, and the blessings of *all* your relations?

When do you take a moment out of your precious time only to smile at someone who is having a harder day than you? Do you know that a smile is worth an offering of a thousand flowers of bright and fragrant colors?

And when do you take the time to appreciate the alchemy of each precious lesson presented to you, only to say:

Are you awake, my dear?

Are you living your dream or merely dreaming it?

*M*erging Divine Feminine and Divine Masculine 1

I love flowers.

They achieve the perfect union of masculine and feminine by the mere fragrance of their being.

Very few can achieve this, even after lifetimes of spiritual sadhana.

Merging Divine Feminine and Divine Masculine 2

A woman is the womb of the world.

Everybody went through the womb, no exception.

Think about this: when you die, you die alone. Even if you are surrounded by your loved ones and are greeted by loved ones on the other side, at the time of death, you still have to go through the doorway alone.

But when you are born, you are not alone.

As you are sucked through that narrow passage, the black hole singularity, the pull of spirit into matter, the conduit, the doorway has already been made for you. Not only has it been made, but it has been nurtured, cherished and loved.

Then, for 9 months, you are built, fed, loved and nurtured with every breath and every thought of your mother.

This is why men cannot understand creation the way a woman does with every cell of her body.

And this is why merging the feminine and the masculine, the activation of our entire DNA, is a key to integrated oneness.

How do you put that into practice?

By being strong yet flexible,
Firm yet yielding,
Open and receptive
Yet giving and generous,
Patient yet commanding,
Humble and yet unashamed of your beauty.

Self-Acceptance

We rarely acknowledge when we fight with parts of ourselves. Most of the time, we are not even aware of it. But what we feel instead is resistance, discomfort and discontent; and we manifest fighting and hardship on the "outside."

When we finally accept ourselves, in all our dimensions and for all that we are, what a relief!

We are finally free, and that is the quality we generate, no matter what outer circumstances come our way.

Individualized Particle of God

You are individualized particle of God.

You are the seed of oneness made manifest through the blooming of your own unique expression – your unique personality with all of its quirks, all of your talents, all of your challenges designed to bring out the best in you.

Even all of the ways you still believe that you don't deserve love and happiness, is only endless expression of the Divine reflecting on itself on its way back to oneness.

To find the Divine within, there is nothing to "do".

I only suggest the practice of stillness because I find endless gifts in it.

I also find endless inspiration in great saints and great teachers and I don't want to just practice their wisdom. I want to practice what they practice – the practices that opened them up to that wisdom.

Remember, I suggest seven minutes of stillness to make it easy to accomplish and enjoy. I don't want anyone to escape in their heads and cultivate boredom or frustration, as may happen with inexperienced practitioners if they "try" to meditate for too long.

Seven minutes is enough to have your life reviews, your "ah-ah" moments. However you must have the courage to empty your cup, because the more you force and try, the less it happens. The surrender in silence is the blissful experience – the dissolving of all busyness and limitations back into the vastness of your original nature.

Other thing you will easily recognize is that there actually is no real separation of time that says, "oh, I've been through my day, now I'm meditating." Such separation is only artificial separation created by the mind. In reality, time is not what you think it is. There is only this present moment of continually expanding awareness – only you present with yourself, whether your attention is turned inward or outward.

So let's say you have an awakening experience during your meditation, which is like seeing a point of light. Now that point of light changes your perspective on the rest of your life, and you have embarked on a journey of self-discovery.

As you allow that point of light to expand in duration with your dedicated practice, you reverse the balance; eventually, your meditation is not the peak of your blissful awareness but your everyday life becomes the light of your consciousness that shines forth as the love, the joy and the grace that you carry.

Each time you let go of layers of conditioning caused by hurts and neglects, you get closer to who you really are, in great simplicity.

Everyone comes in as a point of light and starts gathering experiences in the womb and at birth. We were all born as bundles of love and tenderness with perfect potential for joy, outrageous creativity, capacity for learning and self-expression.

*W*orld *Peace 1*

Peace begins in your heart.

First, imagine you can achieve world peace in your heart.

If you think this is too big of a task, what are we going to accomplish really?

Accept that this universe is one. Accept that it wants your joy, abundance and freedom because this is what the universe is made of; and you are it, a child of the universe.

Accept that for every atom and every cell of your body, there is a universe out there that matches it, responds to it, reflects that fraction of the light that you are made of.

Everything else is stories, all designed to bring us back home, right there where we started: in the heart, as joy, peace and freedom.

This meditation I offer you first came to me as I am doing my daily practice. I can only give what I practice, and nothing else. Please translate it in your own words. Empty your cup and see what truth wants to flow through you.

Meditation:

No thought.

Blissful state.

No worries, no thinking. Nothing to fix, nothing to figure out. Smile and just BE.

From emptiness, the quantum void of all possibilities, the question will always arise:

What does my soul want right now?

Do not rush for answers; continue to empty in silence so you build up more bliss and more light.

Let this light bring you back to emptiness, only this time, you are bathing in light.

Whatever story comes up, follow that story until it brings you back home, my dear.

There is a place well beyond joy. This place exists also in your heart.

God is what's left after you empty all the stories.

Come back to your personality, only now because it has touched grace, it now reflects a fraction of the light. You see that everyone you've ever met is like a mirror of multi-dimensional colors, each reflecting their own beauty.

Every single lesson is a reflection of you. Do you see that my dear? You are home, always have been. Where else could you be?

Your mind is like a fractal that traces back all your history at the speed of light, through all your dimensions that exist simultaneously. As you line them up through the window of your perception, you realize that all this time you were already home.

Oh Divine Splendor, how can I forget you?

Of all the stories, isn't this one the most magical – to merge with infinite love?

And now I cry like a baby, Oh God of Infinite Sweetness. Why all this grieving every time I open my heart to infinite light?

Oh yes, another story to follow to its source.

I grieve my losses and disconnections.

Yes sometimes, I equate love with grief because it is what broke my heart open in the past.

So when my heart breaks open in the moment, it has the memory of grief instead of joy.

But love is joy, so you transmute the feeling of grief into joy – the joy of infinite love not bound by time, space, life or death.

Dear reader, whatever story brings you back home, that is the one you want to follow.

That is the path of returning home, of merging the ending with the beginning.

The path of the one expanding into infinite diversity, only to return back to oneness – exuberant all-encompassing oneness.

Remember now, you are not the story. You are the space that contains it.

It is a very special kind of space: it has no boundaries, no limits – well, at least I cannot see it.

You are also the void at its center. That's why this space has no limit, like a torus that swirls back unto itself in an infinite fractal pattern of division expansion (picture a bit like those Klein bottles[8] that close on themselves, except make it 5 dimensional if you can – the 3 familiar dimensions of space, plus one hidden dimension[9] so that space can curve unto itself, and one dimension of time which is, as you remember, completely interchangeable with all the dimensions of space).

Now my dear, dear friends, let's drop the stories one more time, and begin our meditation. Shall we?

It goes like this: Empty your thoughts, smile and just be. From emptiness, the question will always arise…

---

[8] *You may be more familiar with the Moebius ribbon, which is a twisted figure 8 ribbon that has only one side. If you follow one side of the ribbon all the way, you will end up on the "opposite" face without having to cross the edge. The Klein bottle is a sort of 3-D equivalent of the flat Moebius ribbon. It is a bottle whose inside merges with its outside: it contains itself.*

[9] *To put it simply, if you want a line (1-D object) to close on itself, it has to exist in 2-D space so you can close the line in a circle. So to close a 3-D space on itself, it has to exist in a 4-dimensional space.*

The Mirror of Relationships

Have you noticed how others are a reflection of what you believe about yourself?

Nobody can make you feel a certain way unless that seed of feeling wasn't already there within you – sometimes lying dormant in your subconscious, simply waiting to be activated and released.

So it's okay to be mad or disgruntled if you must. After all, you also help others learn about themselves with your fierceness and truth. But make sure to take the time to be thankful and to honor one another.

In the end, it comes down to this. The choice to be happy is yours. Nobody else is in charge of your happiness. Spirituality 101 is don't give your power away, and take it back if you have.

To give your power away means to put the source of love outside yourself. How, then, can you have love to give?

Instead of giving the keys of your happiness to someone else, how about a sweet prayer like this to bring you back to center:

Nectar of my heart, God, Deity, Guru, whatever form my small mind can represent, you are always present within myself!

Then be the giver of joy, not the one grasping for it!

Would you be surprised if I told you that the easiest and most effective way to detangle yourself from old subconscious programming and to remember who you are, is to spend some quality time with yourself?

Remember, we are always connected in this holographic universe. We are vibratory beings who are always sensing others' vibrations, thoughts and feelings. As we honor each other's reality, clear of our own energy signature, we can come together and make those beautiful iridescent interferences patterns[10] – the product of our realities merging and creating new ones.

---

[10] *When two waves (patterns of vibration) cross each other, they create a new pattern of vibration (called an interference pattern) that is more than just two waves taken separately. This principle is at the basis of holograms, hence the name of the "holographic" model of the universe.*

*P*aths to the Divine

In spiritual practice (regardless of tradition), there are two kinds of experience.

First there are the peak experiences. I call those candies of the universe to let you know you're on the right track, and to encourage you on your path.

The best attitude is to see those as side effects. Don't grasp for these experiences and don't get attached to them; this only creates blocks. Think about it: an experience occurs only once; everything happens in its own time, so why rush?

After the peak experiences comes emptiness. Peak experiences become rare, because they have become your new normal.

However that emptiness is *the* peak experience. It is the oneness, the bliss born of itself, the nectar of all manifestations. It is the formless of infinite potential, the energy of creation.

Make that emptiness vibrant with one-pointed devotion (pure love), and the whole universe opens up to you, or whatever your heart desires.

This is very practical believe it or not. If you use spiritual practice as a way to escape life, it will make you unhappy or unbalanced, just like anything else. This is why all of my teachers emphasize grounded spirituality.

The best way to open up is to have a good life. Take care of things and responsibilities, and nurture your creativity and special talents that only you can give to the world. Sing, dance, paint, write your own prayers in your own unique way.

Sing your own song to the Divine; this is infinitely more valuable than mindless repetition of someone else's prayer that you have not learned to make yours anyway. Once you have made your own prayers, you will understand others' because you will see that they are the same.

Stay simple. Remember, your best teachers are those closest to you. Who else has the courage to show you a true reflection of all of you?

That's the mirror of relationships. Notice how the parts of us that we haven't learned to love and accept will inevitably come up as pairs of matching opposites with our partner.

Issues will match like a lock and a key. Wherever we have resistance, the blocks will surely point their nose up and secretly scream, "Please take care of me!"

That is the healing power of relationships designed to bring us back to wholeness.

The sooner we recognize that our blocks are the result of earlier conditioning and survival imprints, including unresolved issues passed on through generations, the quicker we can make each other allies on this journey back to wholeness.

That is the healing power of relationships.

Relationships, honoring one another is the highest spiritual path I know.

Not just intimate relationship, but any relationship is the path to the Divine.

*E*mbracing Our Limitations

If we are light, why do we forget?

I suppose, as I have written before, that it is because a beam of light in empty space doesn't know it's light until it has something to reflect on.

Remember, you are both the light and its source, the empty space of infinite potential popping into existence – who knows why? I call that the Great Unknown. Simply keep a childlike sense of wonder and awe at the great mystery of which you are the embodiment!

Your capacity for love is, and always has been, intact. Even the hard lessons are the way our soul is tearing us apart so that we can stop all the games of pretense (such as pretending to be broken) and remember who we are.

If you doubt, just love somebody; do random and daily acts of kindness, just for the fun of it, because it is more fun to spread joy and make others smile than to give in to collective doom and apathy.

Love yourself; do what lights you up. When we love ourselves, love overflows.

If your reality reflects to you a lack of love, consider this as a gift showing you where you are holding back the flow of love. Smile, say thank you, and return to the most simple form of loving yourself just the way you are – accepting yourself just as you are now with all your amazingness and so-called imperfections.

Accept your challenges as part of the ingenious design of your soul wanting to get your attention and bring out those special gifts that you and only you can give. It is through overcoming our challenges and following our deepest aspirations that we get to shine, uplift and inspire others.

When you say yes, the universe will present you with constant opportunities to love.

Have you noticed that the most physically challenged persons are often so bright in spirit? I have a friend who broke his spine from falling from a tree. He has been stuck in bed for seven years, quadriplegic, body all bruised and sore from inaction and being stuck in bed day and night 24/7, 365 days a year.

He says, "I never have an angry thought, I never complain, I always try to stay positive."

When I visit him he always greets me with a huge smile. I often remind him, "You're a hero; you should write a book. People have a lot to learn from you.

I think the best way to teach – in fact, the only way to teach – is by example, by simply being yourself.

Growing up, I used to think there was something wrong with me, that I wasn't normal – I often experienced anxiety or discomfort that I could not comprehend nor put into words.

By the time I reached my teenage years, I was seriously withdrawn, virtually autistic (although I have never been diagnosed as such).

I can be very warm, funny, joyful, caring and connected; and the next day be grumpy and unable to communicate and connect (to the great frustration of my (ex-) wife).

I must say, however, that I have been blessed by her continuous support and radiance during this next phase of my journey.

Of course, I have become much more comfortable with myself over the years; otherwise, I would not be here sharing with you.

But yes, I do take things literally. Yes, I have perfect and instant memory for all the things I care about and feel connected to but can be utterly ignorant and forgetful about the things I consider of no importance. Yes, I can be awkward and uncomfortable in social situations and I've never liked parties very much.

When I was a kid, I was extremely sensitive to meanness, cruelty, injustice, hypocrisy, any form of manipulation; and I gradually withdrew as a way to protect myself.

I could see in my family – close and extended – that unhappiness was rampant, but one never talks about those things and must all agree to smile and pretend that everything is just fine.

The negative side of my self-protection mechanism is that over the years, while growing up, I increasingly avoided personal feelings and interactions. Yet, I allowed deeper feelings of love to have an outlet in astronomy, music and rock climbing.

When I was 18, my mother had a sudden nervous breakdown, the result of accumulated unhappiness in her life. She attempted suicide, and received electroshock treatments that did wiped out both her depression and her personality. While in recovery, she fell on a set of stairs and died from head injury.

I spent the next seven years in complete isolation. I was a physics student at university and could not maintain my attention in class; I would often doze off instead. During final exam time, stress would push me to study a week, or even sometimes just the night before the tests. I was unable to relate to any of my classmates, except for one friend who I introduced to rock climbing.

What helped me survive this deeply alienating time of my life, and be able to come back (still today I consider it a miracle, it always makes me cry) is that I maintained this passion for rock climbing. In particular, while I was doing my doctoral work in the South of France, I would spend all the time I could in nature, hanging by my fingers on the vertical walls of the beautiful cliffs of Provence. It also helped me to relearn to connect with others and make some very good friends, although I did make sure to keep some distance to hide that deep sense of alienation. That is, until a breakdown pushed me to start changing that pattern.

Much of my life's theme has been learning to get out of my shell, and by extent of experience, helping others who have the same desire to do so.

I can honestly say that every hardship, every breakdown has been the blessing that has pushed me to open up.

It is very hard to see this while in the midst of the hardship, but over time, immense gratitude emerges out of all the changes that have been allowed.

Shortcomings 1

We all at times get careless with our words.

Carelessness comes when we approach our limits, in moments of stress, exhaustion, anger, fear or selfishness.

This usually causes a situation to worsen; and the situation will either fall apart and get a chance at being corrected later, or it will simply completely dissolve.

The best attitude is to live without regrets. Never say something that you will regret later and when it's too late.

I, too, lose it at times; but one thing I've learned is to let go of stubborn pride, acknowledge my shortcomings, and make things right by shifting attitude and apologizing in words and actions as soon as I can.

Shortcomings 2

Every full moon, I do special practices, breathing method and I fast for three days. I skip the fast if I'm not in the mood, have low energy, or have a lot to deal with.

But because of this special full moon, I did fast even though I was already very tired.

After two days of exhaustion, I suddenly have enormous energy. I had a double load of teaching piano lessons today without any break (because I had to cover for another teacher needing the time off). I stayed inspired and present all the way.

I feel so clear.

I'm reminded how we often use food to fill an emotional void rather than to get more energized.

Also, after fasting you feel so clear that the last thing you want to do is put junk food in your body again.

But the most valuable benefit from this fast is that another layer of judgment is lifting. Last week, I had a little fall out with a very dear friend who got upset with me when I thought I was being friendly.

I can now see clearly that every conflict I experience is not because the other person is being mean to me; but rather, because I am being judgmental of their behavior and because of some shortcoming on my part I was not willing to face.

So if somebody appears mean to me, I have two choices: I can fight it and perpetuate a whole lot of drama, or I can say, "wow, thank you for showing me where I am still holding blocks." Only courageous and fierce people will reflect truth as opposed to merely being nice and polite, so it is my learning to be graceful about it.

Interestingly, after this experience, I came across the following quote of His Holiness The Dalai Lama:

> *"Seeing one shortcoming in oneself is more valuable than seeing 100 in others."*

*F*acing Our Fears

(Transmuting Fear Back Into Grace)

A fearless person is not one without fears, but one who can embrace them and turn them into something golden.

Facing our fear is not as easy as everyone wants to believe.

To face our fear, we have to stop running away from it and actually feel it. No matter what we say, it is natural to avoid fear; we all have spent a lifetime running away from it to some extent.

Paradoxically, the seeds of fear that we push away in our subconscious will magnetize and create those situations that will mirror those fears back to us. This is the drive built into our very nature to bring us towards healing and back into wholeness.

Facing our fear is an unavoidable step on the spiritual path.

My teacher says for every step into the light, we do one step into the dark.

Another analogy I've heard is, let's say you are used to a 20-watt light bulb to light up a huge warehouse; you don't see much. When you open yourself up, you increase your energy. So now, it's like having a 1000-watt light bulb. Suddenly, you see a lot more, and you get to see all the clutter that was previously hidden.

The sages say in symbolic language: when the monsters (your fears) catch up with you, stay still and let them swallow you and spit you out (metaphor for your transformation).

The following is from a meditation I recorded in my journal some time ago.

The easiest part to write was the invocation prayer. The rest is subjective direct experience – to allow waves of feelings and to return to stillness – most of which cannot be put into words.

The whole session – prayer, stillness, waves of feelings, surrendering deeper into stillness and back and forth – was about one hour.

You must understand the whole thing is spontaneous (as is everything else in this book); there is no one way to do this.

The only reason I share this is to encourage you, if you are experiencing recurring fears, to use stillness (or whatever it is that you do or that you *stop doing*) in order to bring yourself back to your center. Embrace your fear until it transmutes into peace and love, which is at the root of everything, always.

...

Dearest God of Grace and Light, Infinite Sweetness, All Encompassing Wisdom and Understanding, Both form and formlessness, highest vibration within my heart that therefore I hereby summon, highest within the heart of all saints and all great souls,

As I am here to confide in you my tiny problems, I must humbly first ask you to ease the suffering of all your children on planet Earth. May all overcome the hardships they endure and be brought back safely into Love.

Please raise my vibration, purify my emotional body and karmic body that I may respond from love and care, so that I can be a safe harbor back into love for others.

Dearest God of Infinite Light, please ease my burden of fear and worries that I may serve in love, caring, connectedness, resourcefulness, in whatever form my soul is capable of and by your grace.

Dear God of Infinite Grace and Light, please teach all of us to treat ourselves with kindness, love and softness.

May we all treat ourselves with kindness, self-love and softness;

And therefore treat others with kindness, love and softness.

Dearest God of infinite grace, I am begging at your feet, please remove fear and separateness from my mind and remind me of the ways of love, I beg of you.

Dearest God of infinite sweetness, since there is absolutely nothing I can do to hear you or see you or get closer to you, I will now descend deeper into my body, into my heart, into my belly, into my breath,

And surrender into the emptiness of silence, no matter how scary or uncomfortable it may seem.

Layers of grief...

Return to silence, more vibrant every time.

Just staying still with the feeling. Not trying to change it. Neither making it stronger nor making it go away. Simply be with it and remain still...

Sudden clarity.

Oh God of infinite grace, you are doing your infinite play within myself, since all I perceive, understand, interpret, all of it happens within myself.

All my love and devotion happen within myself.

All my worries and concerns happen within myself.

Even my understanding of distant stars happens within myself.

There is nothing that I can see that is not a projection of you on the surface of my mind,

There is nothing that I can feel that is not the living pulse of the universe beating through my heart....

Wow...I cannot explain but all fear of outside events out of my control suddenly disappear, leaving space for incredible peace – the peace that can shower everything on the outside, bless everything as it arises, bless everyone I encounter, no matter what outer form and appearance.

Oh, thank you God of infinite grace for this sweetest realization and experience of oneness.

I will one more time melt at your feet in the form of silence and stillness...

If I could clarify this insight, it's never that any outside situation is scary; it is me who projects that label, that feeling into it, which doesn't help at all.

Once the projection is dismantled, all I have to do is project/beam peace, kindness, softness... and watch the miracles unfold.

And this is how a prayer is answered.

On Grieving

When you miss, let yourself miss,

When you ache, let yourself ache all the way,

When you cry, it does not matter if it's a single tear or a torrent washing over you.

Little by little, you will see that each tear becomes a Jewel refracting the multi-colored light of the Divine;

And that there really never was that much separation between life and death;

Just enough to create those beautiful stories while we are here, on our way back to wholeness.

And when the aching is too much, know that you are always, always welcome in the arms of the Beloved.

R̲eleasing Old Subconscious Programming

First, I want you to understand that there is nothing you have to do to release old subconscious programming. (There you go, the pressure is off.)

In particular, do not waste time with years of therapy, rehashing the same old stories and living in the past. This may end up reinforcing the stories that drag you down instead of getting rid of them. (Of course, this is not to discount the immensely valuable service that a therapist can provide in terms of support, healing, coping skills and encouragement in critical times.)

But you must understand that these things (some call our shadows) have a timing of their own, as you can experience in your own life. They come back in cycles as we progress on the spiraling ladder of self-discovery. (This mirrors the cyclic revisiting of emotional programming that has been stored in our DNA – which is, as you know, shaped as a spiraling ladder. As we evolve "upward" the spiritual path, we unravel deeper "down" into the old programs still stored in our DNA.)

You cannot pray yourself out of an old programming. You cannot goodwill neither rationalize yourself out of it. You cannot talk yourself out of it (and even much less talk anyone else out of it).

However, when you get stronger, the universe (your soul, your higher-self, the simple law of cause and effect – it's all connected) will say, "oh, you are ready; now is a good time to revisit this old issue and let go of another layer." Of course, things are not happening in a vacuum. Things will happen in your life. You will think of those things, those "triggers" as overwhelming or bad. This is where you have to be smarter than your own defense mechanisms.

Since you are embracing more light, whatever does not match it comes to the surface to be released. It has to be symbolized onto something; it has to appear real (otherwise, it would feel even worse; it would feel like you are just losing it).

It will feel awful, like pus coming out. Since the old program was put in, it will feel similar when it comes out. But you survived the first time, so you will survive this time.

The tricky part is to not focus on the awfulness. Trust in your own process, the wisdom of your soul guiding you, or the benevolence of this universe, or God's unconditional love. Use whatever works for you – all are true.

And you have to ride the wave with the least resistance. Dive into it. Let yourself be engulfed by it. Fighting it only delays the healing.

If you have gotten that far, it is essential that you do not stop until you come to peace, to some kind of resolution. So it will take fierceness, determination and honesty on your part.

I have been so transformed by the healing I'm about to share. As a result, I am more deeply relaxed in my own beingness, without having to earn it or deserve it or work at it, but just because I am.

Remember, this only took one session, not years of therapy. This is why you cannot plan it, nor force it to happen. The baseline of your meditation is to smile, keeping a gentle focus on your breath to help you get out of the head. Focus on what you want. Then rest in the bliss of your own nature; or, if you have experienced that stage already, the next stage is to rest into the emptiness of your own nature, the space of clarity.

Sometimes, I write my meditation journeys as a way to hold a mirror to myself and give myself focus. So here is what I wrote:

After running so much energy, having visions of light, praying to the divine over and over, emptying my cup, melting in bliss of divine realization, experiencing fractal visions of creation of time and space, and having an outpouring of creativity, tonight I really crashed into grief.

Overwhelmed with grief. Nothing else I want to do but dive into this grief; let it take over.

If I really listen to my body, I have this enormous ache swelling up in my belly. I can't even remember when this grief started; it's preverbal.

I'm crying, coughing and choking as if a hairball wants to come out of my throat; and nausea is swelling up from my belly.

Grief of failures, grief over the cycles of connection and disconnection. Grief over not knowing how to take good care of myself.

Grief of all losses.

Grief of losing myself.

Where did it start? In the womb? At birth? When my older brother, who hated me so much, tried to strangle me as an infant?

(As a side-note, this concerns only my emotional processing and bears no judgment on my brother for whom I have only love. The brother I talk about here is only a small child and a thing of my past. He expressed his feelings the best way he knew how, considering his reality at the time; just as I expressed my feelings the best way I knew how, considering my reality at the time.

In general I avoid talking about others but I don't see how I could share this emotional processing with you without sharing a minimum of context.)

When did I separate from myself and say: "I got to hide and make myself invisible to survive; I got to withdraw deep inside to protected myself?" So of course my life is under the sign of grief.

Stillness (I return to silence and stop making anything happen; I only smile, breathe and wait)

Yes, I have always thought of myself as "less than" and unworthy because of the way my brother looks at me.

I have no rancor against him really. I am only looking at this deep programming within myself.

(After this healing, I can even say more than that. I have immense gratitude for the beauty of my brother's soul for being willing to play that part in giving me such depth of learning in self-love and compassion.)

Oh Master of love and compassion, how do I stop seeing myself as such – unworthy and less than?

How do I see myself as valuable as any human being?

What could I tell myself that would convince me of this?

I could say, "Christophe, you are just as valuable as any human being," but still, deep down, I still see myself as unworthy and less than.

I beg your mercy, Lord of love and compassion, show me the reason for this belief so I may transmute it into liberation.

When I close my eyes and return to stillness, I can hear the voice of my brother saying, "you are less than any other human being I have ever seen on this planet; you are the most stupid I have ever seen." Those were the repeated words I grew up with and ended up completely believing.[11]

But today, I can smile and see that it is not truth, but only a reflection of his pain, of his own suffering. If I could free myself, I would also free him from playing this role.

So I will now concentrate on freeing my brother… Stillness

That's a big one. I cannot free him from his pain. That's between him and his soul. But I can free him of the energetic attachment he had of making me the cause of his suffering and unhappiness

---

[11] *An example. As a teenager I loved gymnastics and was very good at it. I decided to join a class. On the first day, I was so self-conscious and feeling stupid that when the others in the class looked at me doing my first exercise, a simple cartwheel, I fell flat on my back. They laughed and someone joked that I should try bicycle instead. I can't blame them. This is pretty funny in retrospect and such a good example of how we recreate our predicaments.*

So others were not mean, just merely playing the part I gave them in my scenario. So I encourage you to reflect what scenario do you repeat over and over and what part do you make others act out in your play?

(losing the exclusivity of mommy's love and attention; needing to have his feelings heard and understood; needing to be comforted and reassured, but not receiving it). I can free myself from the energetic attachment of playing victim for him.

Wow! Could it be that simple? Now when I look at that statement – "I am less worthy than any human being," – it becomes empty. It makes absolutely no sense. I can't even imagine what that could possibly mean.

Wow! Could I be free of that belief? God of infinite grace, help me remember who I am, even if at times I completely forget.

At the same time that I can hear my brother tell me I am the most stupid on the entire planet, I pray to God, to the gracious light of infinite love, to please free my brother of his hatred, and the enormous pain and suffering he must be feeling underneath. I really wish for that. My brother must be suffering so badly. Please, ease his burden; please, bring him back to love – not for me but for himself. I beg of you, dear Lord of grace. You see, I am actually okay. I have not completely lost touch with love and compassion, so it is not for me that I pray. Maybe I am completely deluded, but I think it makes sense. Even badly treated, a child will still have compassion and feelings for how disconnected from love an authority figure can be.

And this is where I remember who I am. I doubt I have dismantled all the layers but at least I can say now:

I am just as worthy as any human being.

I am worthy of showing who I am.
I am worthy of sharing who I am.

I am worthy of letting my love, my joy, my creativity reach out and touch other people.

Closing Prayer – O God of Infinite Grace, you reside within me as peace, love, joy, compassion, wisdom that I put in service for the highest good of all. Thank you.

*O*rdinary Miracles

Self-love and self-transformation are the rules of the game.

You cannot practice love; that is not love. You *are* love.

You cannot practice compassion; that it is not compassion. You *are* compassion.

You can only be yourself.

Your soul is already pulling you exactly where you need to be, doing what you do.

The most simple, authentic surrender will reveal that. In the meantime, we have so much fun thinking we are the doers and we make things happen. In truth, they are already happening. All we have to do is get out of the way, so to speak, and the magnificence of the whole universe can run its course without obstruction.

Everything will take care of itself for the best when we step out of the way. The way is what wants to happen, what is already happening.

Now practice that, because the universe will constantly throw at you a mirror of your disbeliefs so that one by one, you can peel them off and remember that there is only magnificence unfolding.

Then you can watch miracles of transformations respond instantly; it will blow your mind. At this point in my journey, miracles have become quite ordinary. Most of them are just too personal and may not be of much interest to you. But I will share this one simple example:

It's very hard to find housing on Maui at the moment. I am talking about many months of search without success. With only 10 days' notice at my current place, my only committed prospect suddenly pulled back on me at the last minute.

Instead of going into stress and anxiety, I practiced staying in joy and trust that whatever wants to happen is already in the making. As my energy lifts (and I act accordingly), three unexpected and wonderful opportunities show up.

How much fun is that?

Find the balance between the being and the doing (in this example the surrender with trust into higher guidance, and the acting on that).

Find the balance between details and overview. The sphere of non-duality does not discriminate. We easily get caught up in outer appearances. It's understandable. When you watch a movie, do you see the images or the clear screen that is behind it? Take time everyday to listen to silence, and enjoy. Trust me your soul will thank you for it.

(P.S. I now live in a perfect artist musician spacious studio in the middle of the beautiful and secluded jungle of Twin Falls.)

The Middle Path

The middle path, as I see it, may not be the same as what you think it is.

Otherwise, I would not bother writing.

In my experience, the highs are not separable from the lows.

When I'm high on life, and I surrender to exquisite bliss during meditation, joy will suddenly bring this deep crying of appreciation (similar to the kind of cry at the good ending of a movie).

When I'm low and I have no choice but to surrender on my knees, a new depth of understanding will suddenly emerge out of nowhere and shed light on the whole experience, bringing a whole new area of joy and expansion. It never ceases to amaze me.

So to me, the middle path is not one where I become more numb, but one where I increase my ability to experience a wider range of highs and lows while maintaining my center, my peace, my ability to love.

Please do not think for a moment that I dwell in equanimity, because I don't. But I certainly marvel at this process that constantly pulls me back center no matter what the extremes.

This experience has given me great depth of trust and faith in human nature, no matter what extremes we go through.

Although it is not always easy to maintain inner peace, it does become easier to hold that vibration for those who need it, which is simply to stay in awe at the beauty of each path.

We Are One

I am sure you have your own experience of oneness.

Sometimes it can be very simple and powerful; sometimes so exquisite yet subtle that it can hardly be put into words.

Sometimes, we get glimpses of oneness through synchronicities and answers to our prayers.

I'll share three little stories to encourage you to recognize those moments in your life.

The first story happened the very next day after I had an awakening experience. I wrote about it already in Part 1, but I always enjoy remembering that story.

This happened a few years ago. The experience in itself was nothing extraordinary; it just stands out as a moment where my heart blew open in tears of joy and the shift in perspective felt jaw dropping in the moment. My realization had to do with understanding that there cannot be any obstacle to infinite love; in other words, everything can be met with open heart and unconditionally loving attitude, and with this, one is immediately freed from all self-imposed misery. Only our small mind gets offended or afraid and makes us believe the stories of limitation.

What happened the very next day felt like no coincidence, but direct confirmation of the powerful experience I just had. I unexpectedly came across this beautiful book of poems by Mother Theresa (I did not even know she had written books), and opened the book at random straight to this page:

"The fruit of silence is prayer

The fruit of prayer is love

The fruit of love is service

The fruit of service is silence"

The second story (also in Part 1) happened after I read the beautiful book *The Life of a Saint* about Shree Maa. I was so inspired and moved by her dedication and devotion, I felt drawn to ask her for guidance in my prayers. I often receive an answer when I make my mind truly silent, and the answer pops up all at once, as a vivid and clear insight. I heard this sentence:

"Feel the unifying principle within yourself and in your life."

I felt exquisitely blissful and high from that experience for two or three days. Interestingly, a few days later, I read those exact words (feel the unifying principle), although not from Shree Maa. It may have been from Amma, the hugging Saint, but I cannot be sure, as I do not remember.

Are the messages and insights that come up during meditation suggestions of our higher self, or do they indicate that we really connected with someone else's soul?

I do not worry about these kinds of questions anymore. To me, both realities are true at the same time. To put it into the words of the sleeping prophet Edgar Cayce: all our subconscious minds are connected and are literally one!

The third story, I will call "God's grace in action." I'll simply use the notes from my journal:

"Yesterday, after my oral surgery (I had two wisdom teeth pulled at the same time), and as the numbing shots started to wear off, the pain suddenly became excruciating; I felt intense throbbing. I made it disappear in a few seconds simply by remembering God's name. It was exquisite just to see it work.

Later, when I picked up my prescription, the pharmacist looked grumpy, like she had a bad day. I noticed the old program in me: I'm a bother, things will go wrong, insurance won't cover it, etc. Then I remembered God's name and allowed light to shower down on all of us (including the people working there).

When she came back from behind the shelves, I can swear I looked exactly the same and said nothing. She had a radiant smile; her eyes where literally beaming with light. She said to me, "I'm so cold feel my hand." She reached out, so I held her hand for a long moment and it was indeed very cold.

For a few seconds, she connected in the most natural and kind way; and that, to me, is God's grace in action."

When Giving and Receiving Cannot be Distinguished

A few years ago, I met an old Zen Buddhist master.

A friend told me, "You have to meet this person I'm taking care of at the old folks home. She is absolutely amazing. She can see straight through you, see your potential and tell your future. This woman has not been eating for 6 months and she radiates knowledge beyond words. She had her near death experience, but then she lost her large following after loosing her ability to function and becoming extremely frail. She channels 12 personalities (or entities) and refers to herself as 'we.'"

I thought, "great, this sounds like an opportunity to be of service" (of course I was also intrigued and curious). When we see a great teacher, it's easy to have an attitude of grasping; we forget that they, like us, are simple human beings. So, before going to meet her I did my prayers of surrender, to open myself as a channel for healing and guidance.

When I met her, the first thing I did was smile and laugh.

When you meet somebody who knows that we don't know, words are not necessary. You just immediately start laughing and sharing in the bliss.

She said, "Good, it's so refreshing; so many take themselves so seriously in the 'spiritual' community."

Then we looked into each other's eyes and I felt a little awkward. I did not know what to say. She took control and said, "You don't have to lock eyes. So many think when you speak you have to look deep into each other's eyes, but this can be an overstepping of boundaries."

That put me at ease, so I relaxed and looked away.

Then she asked me about various experiences, and everything I said was immediately greeted with a warm feeling of understanding and recognition, such as, "Oh yes, what a blessing," or, "Oh, what a rite of passage!"

Then – and I forgot how this came along – I did or said something healing for her; or rather, I was just radiating joyful bliss from basking in the presence of this wise being. She suddenly had tears running down her cheeks, and felt this aching in her heart; I told her to let it fill with love. Afterward, she said with great vulnerability and gratefulness, "I felt this door open in my heart; I have been waiting for this moment for so many years."

After those tears of tenderness and a little more sharing, I felt all that needed to be said had been said, and the reason for the visit had become apparent and fulfilled. So we said goodbye and I left, feeling incredibly blessed.

Afterwards, I could hardly comprehend or integrate the sweetness and the preciousness of this visit.

Did I bless her, or had she skillfully given me this blessing by bringing out the gift that wanted to flow through me?

(You remember, I did nothing and merely answered her questions or listened.)

Love is a flow. Who is to say who is the giver, who is the receiver?

The Object of Devotion
The Radiance of Our True Nature
The End of Suffering, War and Violence
Or How to Turn Darkness into Light

I will admit, this is quite a long title and it may seem overly ambitious. If you bear with this reading, I hope you will see that it turns out to be quite simple (but not easy sometimes).

People often ask, how can I keep hope in a world filled with so much war and conflict? How can there be a God when there is that much suffering?

Sages say this world is a mere dream, a projection hanging on the surface of our mind.

So I might as well dream my own dream.

This world is also a school – the school of life or the school of unconditional love. In this school there is no failing. It does not matter how many times we fall on our knees; we pick ourselves up and give it our best shot over and over, a little closer to Love each time.

Remember, that Love is inside you and is reflected back to you as every single experience – no exception – until you understand that you are made of Love and nothing else.

So, object means both the purpose (the goal), as well as the point of focus in your present awareness.

You must understand that this point exists only in the moment, in the eternal now.

Quite often on the spiritual path, I hear people say, I have done the work, I have seen oneness, I'm done with this or that issue, I'm done learning from pain and negativity. I should be happy now.

Then something will happen that will push us out of our freshly new (or old) comfort zone. We start to moan and groan, and we say: Why is this happening to me? Or we may start blaming others – *"It's definitely them, I'm very sure it's not me!"*

At the same time, we may find that our old ways of thinking are no longer working to keep us centered and at peace; our old habits no longer bring us comfort and joy, nor relief from our unrest.

We reluctantly understand (not as a mere philosophical abstraction) that life is change.

Once my teacher told me, "When the snake sheds its old skin, he has to learn to let go or it will hold him in his discomfort."

Actually, resisting change is as futile as trying to hold the Niagara Falls with your bare hands.

The paradox is that the more we grasp for happiness, the more it eludes us.

I wrote the following meditation for times when we feel overwhelmed with this world, for whatever reason our mind makes us believe.

...

Dearest God of Infinite Grace and Light beyond all comprehension, please guide me, comfort me and bring forth guides, masters, saints and teachers of unconditional love beyond time and space that can assist me in opening my heart and releasing my fears back into wisdom, the ocean of truth.

Please open my heart, release the grip of the burden of fear, anxiety and insecurities that I may serve your light on planet Earth.

Please open my heart, nothing else is needed – for an inkling of opening shows that *any* situation is better dealt with an open heart.

Dearest Grace of infinite light, I don't know what else to do now but surrender in silence.

Beloved Saints highest within my heart, there is so much violence and hatred on this Earth; please help reduce this useless suffering. How can we remove the seed of violence?

Prayer is not enough. You have to hold others in you heart and in your arms until they remember that they are made of love and they start releasing the poison of hurt and fear that has been put into them.

In exactly the same way I help you let go of your disconnect and pain, and open your heart by holding you in my arms right now.

There is no other way
There is no easier way
There is no shorter way
There is no safer way
There is no more courageous way. Only the fierce of heart will take that road.

Every single person – past, present or future – that comes to mind, first connect with their soul. Then hold them in your heart until they feel and accept your love. It does not matter if it takes only a moment or an hour; do not stop until the love flows.

In the end, you will see that the one who really needs that kind of unconditional love is yourself.

I realize the person I really need to hold in my heart is myself.

I am the one who is resisting, fighting back, running away.

I am the one who needs to hold myself with unconditional love until that love is felt, received and accepted.

Release all pain back into the light of unconditional love and without judgment.

You will be amazed at how easy it is to love others when you love yourself.

Close with a smile and a one-minute silent meditation.

Bring The Mind to Peace

Bring the mind to peace,

by becoming one with the object of its devotion, deep down into your heart.

How could you not have peace when you are one with what you are longing for?

The object of the mind's devotion is its true nature. Whether you call that Buddha state, God, Goddess, Christ consciousness, the true nature of the mind or the simplicity of your true self, does not matter. They all mean the same to me.

The paradox is that you were never ever separated from oneness (even in your most painful moments as well as your most glorious), and you never will be.

All it takes is a moment to remember.

Once the mind is one with its object, you can enjoy the bliss of perfect surrender, the space of non-duality, where there is only perfection unfolding. There is only love or only the perfect lesson to bring us back to love and wholeness.

Many will wait until the moment of death, or after, to let go of the grasping mind and merge with truth.

What a waste of time when such exquisite bliss of existence is our birthright; it is ingrained at the deepest root of our DNA.

So first you bring your mind to peace by whatever mean is necessary.

Then you bring that peace deep down into cellular stillness. Nothing is required but exquisite surrender to your breath and the vastness (emptiness) of this present moment, the quantum point of all possibilities.

Then who knows, where will you take it from there?

World Peace 2

The greatest service we can give to others is the one of returning to our own radiance. This radiance is the formless essence from which flow joy, passionate creativity, meaning and purpose, simple love and compassion.

When we allow ourselves to remember our own radiance, we allow others to do the same without effort, without struggle, without trying to change anybody; we simply become witness to miracles unfolding.

This is my recipe (like so many before me) for world peace, inner peace, peace in our nations, peace in our cities, peace in our lives, peace in our relationships.

*K*eeping Things Simple

Emptiness, just like oneness, bliss or love cannot be taught; it can only be experienced.

So the first thing is to open yourself up to what it is that you really want.

Nothing else is needed, really. And you will not accomplish anything if you are not honest about what it is that you really want.

*P*urification

If you don't want to get your hands dirty,
Who's going to do it?

In spiritual practice, this is called purification.

My best advice?

Patience my friend; patience.

And love, always.

No matter where you are, always keep love in your line of sight.

Mindset

Mindset is the key, whatever endeavor you embark yourself on.

Everything in this book is a key that you can use.

But here, in regards to spiritual practices, I want to share two simple keys, also known as inner secrets.

The first one is your intent, your goal.

Intent is like setting the sails on a boat: where do you want to go, what do you want?

The second key is the vibrancy of your feelings – the love or any positive attribute that keeps you going.

The love is the energy, the driving force that moves you.

In our boat analogy, the feeling is the wind. Without wind, your sailboat cannot go anywhere.

They are many secret mindsets, inner transmissions but personally, I like to keep things simple so I'll keep it at that.

*T*he Dance of Perfection

Unbearable Exquisite Sweetness

Return everything to perfection; I mean *everything*.

You fear, your anger, your frustrations and impatience, your hopes, your regrets, your judgments, your victim consciousness, your ambitions, your smallness and your greatness, your sadness and your grief.

Everything returns to the space of stillness.

If I must say something to satisfy your rational mind, I will say that your soul knows exactly how to present you with the lesson that will (actually has already) help you remember that you are made of love and nothing else; to help you let go of this tight control you try to have on reality, so that you can remember that you are freedom itself.

Do not tell me that this will not transform your life.

I do not know any more radical shift in perspective. All your blocks will have to pass the test of perfection.

I hope you understand that I am not talking about shutting down and making yourself quiet when you want to shout, neither am I talking about a perfection that is controlling, rigid, judgmental and obsessive. I am talking about a perfection that is all embracing, a perfection that is the ultimate self-surrender, as in falling into the arms of Love herself.

And when you uncover the wealth of life force that is your birthright, you know exactly when to say yes and when to say no, when to act and when to step back. And nobody will have to tell you what is right for you, for you have touched the light herself.

Remember, this is lifelong learning. I am a mere beginner stumbling my path. As you know from your own experience, even your most sublime awakening is only the first day of the rest of your life.

Be patient and kind to yourself and with others.

$\mathcal{T}$he Dance of Perfection

Practice: 7 Minutes of Stillness

Allow the Dance of Perfection to enter through the Door of your Perception!

May Love, Joy, Playfulness, outrageously alive Creativity bursting with Laughter and Play, mutual Understanding, deep Compassion in acts of Kindness relieving suffering of all kinds...

May all this or better prevail on Earth in the spirit of Oneness and Universal Love.

You must understand, dear reader, that I am just a regular person, with my own set of challenges; and if I can see perfection then so can everyone. All I want is to inspire you to that which is highest within yourself and remind you that with dedication, everything is possible.

Perfection, the perfection of your being, the perfection of existence, the perfection of the great mystery unfolding through you, the perfection of your soul journey, I cannot put into words. I do not how to combine all into one the multi-faceted colors of the rainbow: truth, simplicity, exquisite bliss beyond form, heart-melting love and compassion, the recognition of oneness between all souls, the beauty of each lesson. Much of it is revealed through patience.

Most of us want perfection now, so we struggle, we force, we moan and groan, and perfection eludes us. So patience – not a little patience, but infinite patience – is the key. As I often say, the spiritual path is filled with paradoxes. When you truly surrender to infinite patience, time disappears and the whole universe is suddenly at your fingertips.

To see perfection, you have to invite it. It will not suddenly knock at your door if you do not invite it. (Of course it is always there, merely waiting for us to awaken.) How you invite it is by tuning into the frequency of perfection.

Saints of all ages have done it by tuning to silence, by listening to silence. Every spiritual practice I do, including prayer, is a way to allow the mind to return to that space; allow the mind to drop back into the ocean of wisdom, as some traditions call it.

Actually, in silence you will see all religions, all spiritual traditions become one. They are just using different words, different languages. Even separation between believers of this and non-believers of that, becomes meaningless.

So I offer you 7 minutes of stillness. Of course I am not offering anything; stillness is not mine to give. This is only an encouragement that will benefit those who resonate with it.

I suggest 7 minutes because…

… Many of us have busy life and responsibilities, so I don't want to add stress; I want to make it easy to accomplish. If you already have other spiritual practices, this will not interfere; you will still have plenty of time to do your practices or whatever creative work engages you.

… Short meditation time makes it easier to enter the "zone" – no grasping, nothing to fix, nothing to change, nothing to reach for, nothing to figure out; simply tune into the bliss of pure being. You simply don't have enough time to do anything else and you know that if you try to do something other than be still, you quickly waste your 7 minutes of stillness. But that's okay; you can reset your timer and do it again!

For the practice, I suggest the following.

Every evening around 6 pm so that you can tune in to the energy of other practitioners doing it at the same time (don't worry about time zone, your connection is beyond time and space, trust me). Any other time is just as good too. For instance, 6 am is an excellent time for practicing:

> *Create sacred space where you won't be interrupted or distracted. Light up a candle and say a short prayer from the heart stating your intent with feelings. Connect with your highest goal and generate positive attributes within your heart.*

> *Set your timer for 7 minutes.*

> *Sit in a chair with your back straight, close your eyes, and smile. The key is to be still in body and mind: nothing to fix, nothing to change, nothing to grasp for.*

> *Smiling is very helpful: it allows you to get out of the head. It also balances the Sun and Moon channels. When emotions and thoughts settle and balance in harmony, the*

energy can run into the central channel – the channel of clarity. This channel connects the pineal gland (sometimes called the seat of the soul) to the heart (where awakening occurs). Also sitting in a chair is ideal for opening energy channels, and it is comfortable for most people. If you lie down, chances are that you are just going to get sleepy. Lie down only if you have a disability, an illness or an injury that requires it.

At the end of your practice, conclude with an expression of gratitude and appreciation to yourself and for your efforts, in whatever form of prayer is appropriate for you. It may also be helpful to dedicate your efforts to the wellbeing of all.

Remember, it is very important to take regular breaks from practice (for example, 2 days a week, 1 week a month, 1 month a year). There are many benefits to that:

1. Changing routines unhooks us from the patterns and habits we inevitably put into everything we do. When we come back to practicing we have renewed motivation and fresh perspective, rather than just repeating the same old thing.

2. Enjoy the fruit of your practice, which is rest in your spontaneous nature. Everything else will eventually fall away.

3. Many awakening experiences will occur when you are not practicing, because that's when the mind finally lets go.

Also, please don't practice when you are cranky or angry; otherwise that would be the energy you would be cultivating. Or, you could create a groove, relying on practice to fight off those feelings, thereby reinforcing them.

The Cave Retreat 1

This is my practice for the day:

I drink the space of silence,

I feel the liquid bliss so thick running through my veins.

It does not matter how busy I get,

Or how many times I forget.

I can return to the stillness within;

No matter what;

No matter the demands put on me;

No matter the task I set for myself;

No matter what situation I find myself in,

I can instantly return to that state of mind, the divine communion,

All I have to say is

"I drink the space of silence," and watch all the stories dissipate into thin air, leaving only clarity and love.

This is my cave retreat and I am so lucky to share this with you.

(The western world's version of the cave retreat is when life cuts you off from your usual ways, including your definition of yourself! You must understand, how else are you going to transform?)

People embark on the spiritual path full of enthusiasm and dedication, but when things open up, or things get difficult, they don't like it. No worries; nobody does. That's because to open up means to let go of the barricades you have built around your heart to keep yourself safe and protected, and therefore separate.

So please never give up; the universe is very thorough in how deep it is willing to bless you.

Letting Go

I promised myself I would give myself a break tonight – no meditation, no listening to silence, no writing.

Sometimes, my mind refuses to do anything and it's best then that I lie down and do nothing. (Believe it or not, I'm always trying to accomplish a lot and balance many different things and areas of creativity.)

And I cannot help it, in the nothing, the bliss arises; and the more I empty my cup, the more exquisite it feels. So I have to put some of that into words.

Before I understood what "letting go" really means, this concept bothered me.

Actually, many use the expression "letting go" when they want someone else to shut up about their problems – because quite frankly, they have no clue what to do about it.

But true letting go has nothing to do with that; rather, it is the opposite.

True letting go is more of a deep embrace, a letting go of all resistance.

True letting go is the blissful remembrance that there is a divine perfection at work – an inevitable walk towards love, towards the wholeness of our soul; and that our life circumstances and everything that happens on the stage of our life is there for a reason (which, paradoxically is the remembrance of our wholeness).

And with that comes a very deep relaxation, a cellular relaxation and *a letting go of all struggles.*

There is such a funny paradox that the moment one accepts the perfection of our life is the moment it reveals itself as perfect.

Another funny paradox is that we are afraid that if we accept the perfection of our life, it would become stagnant; so we think we have to work hard at things.

But the very opposite is true. Working hard keeps us stagnant and stuck in our routines, while having fun and seeing the perfection of our life keeps us open and flowing, and therefore constantly evolving.

Heartbreaks are just that – the melting of our heart that pushes us to go inward, to break our heart open and remember the deepest truths about love beyond all the stories of limitation.

Heartjoys are the outward expression of our true nature.

Every moment, every encounter, every interaction – no matter how small or how big – is the opportunity to connect with another soul and shine unto their sky.

And all we have to do is be present. Isn't that simplicity pure marvel of existence?

What could be more mind blowing and miraculous than this ability we have to be truly present, day after day, rain or shine?

The Cave Retreat 2

My dear, dear friend,

I can see the light that you hold, waiting for that perfect moment of safety and recognition.

Both you and I know that you have always held that much light.

The nice thing about the cave retreat is that other's opinions quickly fall away.

But the best part, oh, the best part, is when one's own opinions fall away.

And life can be oh so simple and so beautiful, every single moment.

(I have to remind you that the cave retreat has nothing to do with how busy or not busy you are; neither does it involve going into actual cave – although some do.

The cave retreat is when you reach that point when the outer world can no longer give you the answers that you have always been seeking; and your usual distractions no longer work, if not become intolerable.

If you are in a cave retreat, as I know many who are, know that it is your soul at work to strip away what is not you and raise you up to your magnificent self – in truth, simplicity and love.)

The Cave Retreat 3

Be still, my dear friend! Be still.

I cannot put everything into words; I am only a small human. So sometimes I have to use poetry.

Be still. Do not move a muscle. Continually bring the mind back to the goal.

Be still; let the universe wash over you.

And when the universe tramples you, still be still.

From that stillness, that point of light, that emptiness, spirit, essence of who you really are...

Movement, thought, action become one. All is infused with radiant aliveness, exquisite joy and simplicity.

This is the return to the beginning.

Free Yourself Into Truth

What if the greatest blessing was the blessing of yourself?

Contemplating on the great mystery, you cannot possibly think that out of all the eons and eons of existence, you would happen to be alive now, in this particular and infinitely small fraction of time, simply by mere chance, only to return to non-existence.

You must have been here before.

And you chose this particular time to be. Out of all the possible ways to exist – form and formless, as spirit or as incarnate being – you chose to be here, in this particular existence as you!

You see you do not have to do anything to turn your life into the most miraculous blessing.

Just be yourself and speak your truth; the rest will take care of itself. That is how much of a blessing you are my dear.

Love so much, so completely, as if there is no tomorrow.

You never know what tomorrow will bring.

There is only love in the now.

Love what is. Not what was or what should be, but what is.

Love better today than you did yesterday. Forgive yourself and forgive others.

Be the light giver, the generous giver of love and compassion.

Nourish your creativity and your passion. What gets you out of bed, what makes you want to reinvent the world all over again, day after day?

Greet everybody with a big smile. Show them how much you care and love them. Bring out the sunlight they're longing to share.

Over and over, as best you can.

Then you can live a life without regret. No more demons to fight, no hiding in the hope that the world will change for your convenience.

Be happy now.

Giving Thanks

In the celebration of Thanksgiving, there is a great tradition, which is to share what we are grateful for.

Unfortunately, too often we see alarming levels of turmoil on this planet. In many parts of the world there is constant war, along with all the devastations and sorrows it brings. Even in so-called free democracies there is much hardship. So I had to reflect deeply: what does it mean to me to be thankful?

In such agitated times, it would be easy to despair, worry, get overwhelmed with images and actions of violence all over the world, and because of that lose faith in humanity.

First, to lose faith in humanity is the same as losing faith in oneself.

Therefore, I am grateful for humanity. I see every being as a gracious child of the divine, regardless of what they do, what they believe, how they handle life, what their story is (told and untold), and what they remember or don't remember.

I am grateful to every saint who light up my heart with their truth and dedication.

I am grateful for love that created this existence and yours.

No matter how much we externalize violence with judgments, labels, fears and terrors, everything is a reflection on the surface of our mind, and of how much we have realized that indeed, the only reality is love.

For the one who has realized this, there is nothing to fear.

Therefore, I am thankful for every lesson designed to bring me back to truth and wholeness.

I am grateful for every lesson showing me my limits so that I can dissolve them back into infinite love.

I am grateful for my family who shows me what real love is about.

I am grateful for the stars, the moon, for sunrises and sunsets, for blue skies, rain, trees, flowers, oceans and mountains, and beauty everywhere.

I am grateful for acts of compassion bringing relief to all kinds of suffering.

I am grateful for all those who create – artists, visionaries, inventors, passionate people living their art with authenticity.

I am grateful for all those who dare to make a difference, and that is you, my dear, dear friend.

The Inner Journey
Part 3   Returning to the Beginning

Nosedive

My teacher cautioned me not to do too many practices, and to be careful about the nosedive.

Because I was on top of my world, I did not listen.

I thought, I'm having a blast and I know all about nosedive so I can handle anything. Especially after a shaman retreat, I felt like my inner vision opened up to a whole new level. Since then, I have been able to go on soul journeys in which I can go deep down into my subconscious and face deep fears and ingrained negative beliefs about myself, transmuting them through the alchemy of acceptance, love and compassion.

Well, I did nosedive. The not-so-fun kind of nosedive. The deeply humbling kind of nosedive where, once again, all you can pray for is to be able to take your next step and forget all those elaborate plans. The kind of nosedive where all you can pray for is a temporary resolution and relief from your feelings, and then scramble for a few minutes of peace and overview. (I see this as a blowing of the gates, resulting in overwhelm of preverbal memories that were safely buried in the subconscious.)

What gives me the courage to share is that I am still in complete awe at the depth of this soul journey, and therefore I can only be in complete awe at the depth and beauty of everyone's soul journey.

Because I have chosen to let go of formal teaching, and simply teach by sharing who I am, highs and lows, I am free to write anything I want.

My only requirement is that it be a reflection of at least a fragment of the truth that we hold inside, like one color of the full rainbow.

Very few share this kind of vulnerability, which has the effect of transmuting hardships into a gift for others.

It is actually very freeing for me because, deep down, I know everyone goes through highs and lows on their soul journey. So I know what others share and show on the surface is only a fraction of their truth, no matter what they say.

My vulnerability is my strength. I know it creates much hardship for myself, and yet, I would not trade it for anything.

So it is with much love that I thank you for reading.

Wherever you are, never give up. You are love and beauty itself learning to remember and hold the wholeness of your soul in a way you would never have thought is possible.

Meditation Journal

This journal was only for me, but of course now, it is also my joy to share it and make it useful to whoever can use it.

Like I have said many times before, I write first in the intimacy of my meditation. This is why I cannot edit it. Believe me, it would be easier to keep this for myself.

You can observe that my message is the same for years, yet I always express it in new ways because I don't rely on ready-made formulae. I continually empty my cup so I never know what will come up. My output is completely independent of who reads what I write. If I touch only one person, it's enough for me. And if it's only for me enjoying this process, that is enough too.

I already know how beautiful everyone's soul is and the world will do just fine without me.

So my only chance to really move you is to take the risk to be deeply myself and share from the depth of my being what is my unique experience and way of expression.

As soon as I do that, I immediately recognize the depth of your being, the uniqueness of your expression, the brightness of your soul, my dear friend.

So here it goes...

This journal is only for me, I can do whatever I want.

I can choose to make this time of stillness whatever I want.

I choose to look at Love, in whatever form my small mind can recognize.

Love, in whatever form you may, please come abide in my poor heart full of turmoil, fears and insecurities.

Please make all this purification and hard work and all these efforts worthy by reminding me of the truth beyond all efforts and all striving.

My mind can recognize love in many forms in my life, and in silence itself.

What a sweet surrender, to let go of all efforts, all reaching for.

Silence, emptiness is the sweetest. There, you meet all the saints, all the masters.

Surrendering into emptiness is like catching a wave.
You ride the formless, the love, the blissful surrender. Then the

wave takes form into realization, insight or sweet thought. So you surrender again into emptiness, waiting for the next wave.

But the trick is to let go of waiting for the next wave, and instead continually return to emptiness – the sweetest, most simple instruction.

Nobody can fail at it. Yet so few know how to open to it.

It's very simple – either you have achieved emptiness, or you follow the wave of your consciousness until it brings you back to emptiness.

Study all the masters, you will see this is the common root – it is the nexus if you will, the doorway to oneness; or maybe it is oneness itself.

What's needed?

Patience, dedication, persistence, truth, honest surrender to one's true feelings, merging with the object of one's desire, courage and a good sense of humor.

But there I am, teaching again, and getting completely sidetracked!

There is only you sitting in silence – empty yourself once more Christophe.

God of Infinite Love, thank you for making me the way I am.

So uninterested in worldly pursuits and so desirous to merge with truth.

Most people do not understand me, but that's okay; I understand myself.

Oh my God, I am crying again, my heart melting in such tenderness – only seeing a glimpse of golden light.

Only a mere glimpse without form, but the bliss is so sharp I can hardly stand it.

But if I had to give it form, I would say: to all those I have not known how to love, please forgive me. My heart is filled with love for you and it is lifelong learning to learn to express it.

I am back into formlessness. So before returning to stillness, I will focus on sending love into this golden light.

I don't know whether to laugh or cry seeing how much I'm tripping and enjoying the ride. (P.S. As I have written before, I do not do drugs; I enjoy getting my highs naturally.)

I return to stillness – emptiness; only now it is 10 times more blissful.

And I let go of everything. I am only left with exquisite surrender to stillness. How lucky I am that I can offer this to myself, that this is available to me.

God of Infinite Sweetness and Truth, if there was nothing else, it would still be enough for me to melt at your feet in gratitude; except that I am smiling because there is only me sitting in silence.

I know all of this is a lot of distraction isn't it?

You should sit in silence; I promise you, you cannot get bored!

Now seriously, God of Infinite Sweetness and Truth, you see I cannot help it, I cannot keep this to myself. So I beg of you, please give me something tangible that others can use and recognize; otherwise, they will not listen to me, mere imperfect human.

Oh that's a good one! Let go of that layer of clinging and grasping! Let go of getting anything, let go of getting something tangible. Really go down to the core of emptiness – strip of bliss, strip of hoping for, strip of expecting; just stand there.

It does not matter if people do not understand you. Would you want to lower your truth so people understand you or would you rather jump without return into the sea of infinite light?

God I am yours.
I know nothing. I don't know how to do anything well. I don't do grand acts of service.
I hardly know how to get by with this life.
But I surrender into truth with complete abandon.

All tripping has ceased. I start again, here in my body, in the emptiness of this moment, and once more,

I turn myself to love.

She comes to me in the form of a guide that I cannot see and I cannot hear. She says,

> *She is proud of me.*
> *She reminds me to stop trying to break the veil.*

You are here for a reason.
Be fully here. Remember, this life is only a spec in the face of eternity, why rush?
Be fully present on this Earth plane. The rest will unfold from there.
Your mission on Earth is to re-activate the heart flame – the flame of love, of passionate aliveness, of deep compassion, of joy of living and beautiful expression of unique creativity.
Everybody is a shining light but many choose to not remember out of conditioning and trauma.
It only takes a spark for the light to be reactivated, a moment of inspiration. Dare to be outrageously yourself from a depth of truth, authenticity, simplicity as is found deeply within your heart.

...

Perfect timing. My timer just went off. I feel like I came full circle: waves of consciousness – back in my body – emptiness of the moment – specific message to simple joyful presence – feeling deeply relaxed and vibrant.

The Cocoon Phase

The cocoon phase is a necessary stage of transformation. It is the inevitable dying of the old that is no longer working, and the birthing of the new – closer to truth, closer to freedom.

First we resist, because the old self doesn't want to let go without a fight, or at least some aching and moaning.

Just remember, the transformation has already occurred; it is inevitable.

However, because we don't have the corresponding manifested experience yet, we cannot see the benefits; we cannot appreciate the blessings that are still hidden.

Don't rush trying to fix yourself; don't rush trying to resolve your feelings and rehash your old problems.

During this phase, you may have immense craving for sleep, and not be able to do much else. Let yourself rest and heal. Trust that you are rebuilding from the inside, that you are getting "upgraded".

Learn to be comfortable with your growing pains. The less you resist, the quicker the transformation can flow through you.

Everything is Vibration

First I want you to get a little excited and wonder how I am going to make this cliché and overheard statement into something useful to you?

I just saw my amazing friend Fulton. The man just went through his near death experience (doctors gave him three months to live because of a rejection episode after double lung transplant; but I know he will be fine because he has such life force and still has so much to give to this world).

While he was in treatment in recovery at the hospital, he gave himself the luxury of learning Reiki sound healing and even got his certification! That's called making good use of your time.

So I'm reminded that everything is vibration:

When you speak, you create vibration,
When you breathe, you create vibration,
When you are silent, you create vibration,
When you pray, you create vibration,
When you chant, you create vibration,
When you dance, you create vibration,
When you hold someone, you create vibration,

When you love, you create vibration,
When you receive love, you create vibration
When you play and create, you create vibration,
When you rest, you create vibration
When you surrender and accept, you create vibration
When you laugh, you create vibration
When you open yourself up, you create vibration,

And when you listen... you hear vibration.

So you see you are never the victim of your circumstances; you are the creator and co-creator. Your vibrations affect everyone else and everyone else affects you. The only question is what lights you up?

What do you choose to vibrate that lift up others and remind them of the vibration that they want to create?

Fulton reminded me I'm a healer and a teacher. So I laugh and I say, I really don't have my shit together. So he reminds me, that's part of the process, so share that too.

So a healer? Maybe a healer of the psyche, because I continually have to bring myself back center; I continually have to learn to overcome my inner obstacles – everything that maintains the illusion of separation from love in a sort of shock response PTSD everyone is all too familiar with.

When I need to bring myself back center, to return to truth, I ask myself: "What is the vibration I want to create, and what am I going to do about it?"

*F*inding Balance

Have you noticed in your life the constant play of alternating phases of expansion and contraction?

In expansion, we go outward, we do. In contraction, we go inward, we are.

Interestingly, the two phases constantly pull at each other. We get excited with projects; we do and do. We get very busy. Paradoxically, this busyness will create a time crunch; and although we are still busy, we start to contract and tense up.

On the other hand, if we stop the doing, and return to the space of pure being, of going inward, of resting, of healing, we start to feel such spaciousness inside that it will inevitably pull us into our next phase of expansion and creativity.

Allow each phase to run its full expression.

I find balance between the two poles when the doing comes from a place of spaciousness inside.

Drop all the stories. Bring your mind down into your body. And with every breath, relax a little more, unwinding all the accumulated tensions. As you do so, imagine – or better, *feel* – that you are creating space inside your body so that every muscle, every blood vessel, every bone opens up and returns to expansion, to vastness.

When you master this, you will see that the space inside, found in the stillness, is as vast as the whole universe.

Actually, observe how the universe works.[12] Everywhere I see this constant play of expansion and contraction.

----

[12] *As I was writing this, I was reminded of the relationship between the void and black holes. Physicists think that black holes are not black but they radiate energy (Hawking radiation) .*

From interstellar dust, matter contracts to form stars. At the end of its fuel cycle, the star expands. Then it explodes. Its outer shell is ejected into outer space, but the central core remains. If more massive than the so-called critical mass, that core will start to implode onto itself, to collapse (because there is no more fuel to provide the outward energy). As matter is accelerated to the speed of light, mass is converted into pure energy; space and time collapse into a singularity. A fraction of that energy is radiated back out of the black hole to be recycled into the universe.

Now remember, every point of space is the original void, the singularity sustaining the space and time emanated from it. There is no such separation of space and time "here", and no-space and no-time "somewhere else". Think about it, you cannot have "here" oneness, (all times and space collapsed into one), and "somewhere else" (some "other" space and some "other" time). You understand that this is very hard to grasp only because ours minds are so used to thinking "in space" and "in time". The mind is itself the paradox that tries to grasp itself. The two (the space-time continuum and the oneness) are not separate, but coexist as two states of vibration (with, of course, all the degrees in between). One is slow, dense, "in" time, and the other is light, "out" of space and "out" of time. Both states of vibration coexist everywhere and in everyone, and are therefore accessible to all. The space "out there" is a reflection of the space within. Switching realities is very much like changing channels on the radio – literally tuning to another speed of vibration.

If you want to understand nature, go within. If you want to understand yourself, go to nature!

I'm Almost There

I have learned that "almosts" can be hidden mountains to cross.

So I have also learned to never say, I'm almost there.

Everybody knows that "there" is here and now.

But then, you hit the wall and you say, I cannot possibly climb this mountain; and you are deeply humbled.

Then again, one day you notice to your great surprise: Wow, I am on the other side of the mountain. And you realize that it was, like they say, "the blessing in disguise," only a lesson to be learned, a rite of passage. It was your soul patiently, gently or sometimes brutally guiding you towards a letting go of all that is not you.

That is, until the next mountain shows up on your path.

So you might as well learn mountain climbing, or best find that shortcut that will cross straight through the mountain, that "quantum tunnel of de-entanglement."

You drop the stories of limitations and surrender to your soul's wisdom that is guiding you exactly where you need to be, as you, in this moment, holding the promise of infinite possibilities, made manifest through the power of your love.

Align yourself with this love, the love that you are, the love that you feel, and surrender into stillness so that you can touch the quantum-void. Enjoy the ride; it may take you somewhere very beautiful, here and now.

Healers

A healer is someone who has cut through his or her own BS enough that they can help others cut through their own BS.

BS is anything that maintains the illusion of separation from Love, from Source, from God.

Have you noticed that the people who are the hardest to love are sometimes the ones closest to us?

So cut the BS! If you want to see the essence of a person, if you really want to bring out the essence of a person, you have to release all your expectations and judgments, all the mind clutter that has nothing to do with who you really are – and really see that person for who they are.

And show who you really are, because like attracts like. Vulnerability attracts authenticity, love attracts love, BS attracts BS.

Why not start with letting go of self-judgments and expectations, and really see your own essence.

Smile and laugh at how easy things really are when we stop making them so complicated.

Look in the mirror. Underneath all appearances, see your essence in its naked simplicity. Do you like what you see?

Song to the Divine

Oh God of infinite sweetness and truth, I do not care what anybody else says about that, when I speak to you my heart is immediately at home.

You are the sudden inspiration that comes in the form of poetry.

Over and over you show me the deepest truths about love.

Others could say: Who does he think he is? He really does not have his life together and doesn't have much to show for.

To which I would say: That's exactly the point. God has melted my heart so thoroughly at his feet that there is no room left for longing for anything other than radiant truth, radiant sweetness, the nectar of realization, the essence of all things made manifest on the cosmic play of our life and beyond.

Oh God of infinite sweetness and truth, you have taught me the secret language that breaks the barrier – that secret language that is nothing else than the infinite sweetness, the perfect surrender, the melting at the heart into truth beyond words and thoughts.

Oh Dear Reader if only you could understand how literal I am when I say that this secret language is nothing else than that.

Yet, it is also anything that brings you to joy, anything that lights you up, every one of the forms that make you dance, every form that resonates as truth in your heart and then beyond form drops back into the formless ocean of wisdom.

Oh God of infinite sweetness and truth, I do not have enough time with the rest of my life to even begin to utter a single word of the glimmer of the beauty you show me.

Yet here I am making a fool of myself, and being utterly content with it.

Why do you wish that much to free me? What have I done to deserve that much freedom and joy?

Oh yes I remember, this infinite freedom is not something that we earn or deserve; it is who we are, it is the light we are made of, it is our essence dancing free in the formless and yet infusing every form that we touch, manifest or perceive.

Please stop, this is more than my heart can contain. I'm going to start crying again like a baby. How could my heart contain that much joy?

Oh God of infinite sweetness and truth, after all this time, you now give me all that I have longed for all my life. How could I bear that much sweetness?

Song Of Freedom

I have penetrated at the heart of reality.
There is no pretense here
For I am well aware that I have seen nothing (otherwise I would
not dare to say such foolishness)

Yet, that nothing is more luminous than a thousand Suns
More sweet than 1000 lovers' kisses.

This is not meant to compare or diminish anything.
To the contrary, everything becomes entranced with the flavor of
the Divine.
The sight of a flower is subject to ecstasy.
The mere delight in breathing, the sipping in of beingness is
subject to exquisite bliss.

And when the breath is gone and we return to pure essence,
we merge with the Great Mystery; and the Great Spirit pushes us
with a gentle nudge, through the deepest essence of our true desire
saying, let's surrender again to this grand experiment of love, of
joy, of limitlessness that can create whole new universes,

And comes learning to hold the infinite in the world of limitation, of physicality.

Of all your spiritual and vision quests, all your searching, all the teachers saints and gurus who have inspired you, of all the loves you have known, of all the losses you have experienced, of all the conditions you have manifested as the circumstances of your life and as you, dear cosmic child of the universe, of all of this and beyond the tiny arena of our immediate perception, only one question remains:

Are you free?

Are you free to love every invitation of the universe that delights in sending you mirrors of yourself, and that everyone calls this present moment?

Are you free to express yourself authentically with every breath you take and every breath you give?

Are you free to let the energy of creativity run through you with wild outbursts of inspiration?

Are you free to laugh your head off and be utterly, wildly outrageous?

Are you free to grieve when your heart aches, free to grieve when you see the preciousness of life being hurt or disrespected?

Are you free to hurt, and let the energy run through you so that the next moment, even more life force wants to dance through you?

Are you free to reinvent yourself everyday and continually embody more joy, more peace, more wisdom, more love?

Notice that the seed of freedom is already present in each of these questions.

Therefore, the sages say: do not let anything be a problem. Rather, let every perception and every circumstance be self-liberating!